The 4 Ingredient VEGAN

EASY, QUICK, AND DELICIOUS

MARIBETH ABRAMS with ANNE DINSHAH

Book Publishing Company
Summertown, Tennessee

© 2010 Maribeth Abrams
Cover design: The Book Designers
Interior design: The Book Designers
Cover photos: Warren Jefferson, © Book Publishing Co.

ISBN978-1-57067-232-3

Published in the United States by
Book Publishing Company
P.O. Box 99
Summertown, TN 38483
1-888-260-8458   www.bookpubco.com

Printed in Canada

15 14 13 12 11 10   7 6 5 4 3 2 1

Library of Congress Cataloging-in-Publication Data
Abrams, Maribeth.
  The 4-ingredient vegan: Easy, Quick, and Delicious
/ by Maribeth Abrams with Anne Dinshah.
      p. cm.
  Includes index.
  ISBN 978-1-57067-232-3
  1. Vegan cookery. 2. Quick and easy cookery. I. Dinshah, Anne. II. Title. III. Title:
Four-ingredient vegan.
  TX837.A26 2009
  641.5'55--dc22   2009042941

Book Publishing Co. is a member of Green Press Initiative. We chose to print this
title on paper with postconsumer recycled content and processed chlorine free,
which saved the following natural resources:

60 trees
5,658 pounds of greenhouse gases
2,654 pounds of solid waste
19 million BTU total net energy
27,249 gallons waste water

BOOK
PUBLISHING
COMPANY

For more information visit: www.greenpressinitiative.org. Savings calculations from
the Environmental Defense Paper Calculator *www.edf.org/papercalculator*

Shown on the front cover (counterclockwise from the top):
South-of-the-Border Quesadilla, p. 82
Almost-Instant Minestrone, p.37
Melon Balls in Mint Liqueur, p. 124
Chocolate-Covered Strawberries, p. 132

CONTENTS

To Sandra Siskeene.
—Maribeth Abrams

To the Ohio State Crew Club, especially the women's varsity rowers who inspired and critiqued the recipes I contributed.
—Anne Dinshah

ACKNOWLEDGMENTS

Special thanks to Anne Dinshah for recipe development, Tara Smith for recipe testing, Jo Stepaniak for her vision of this book, and to the following people from the Monaco Center for Health and Healing: Celeste Carlton, Lesa McPhearson, and Jack Monaco, MD.

Thank you also to Kristin Bourbeau; Lisa Chandler; Davida Cohen; Kathy Cuomo; Lauri Deary; Amy Diezeman; Brenda Edwards; Gayel Favali; Derek Goodwin; Brian and Sharon Graff; Michael Greger, MD; Stephanie Gundrum; Esther Handelsman; Kim Hoffman; David Keeney; Gerry McMahon; Molly McManus; Phillip Moreland; Christine Papa; Sarah Peters; David Phillips; Elizabeth Reed; Elaine and Aaron Schechter; Rinda Tucker; Diane Wagemann; and Robin Webster.

Finally, my deepest appreciation goes to every member of my family, whose love and support fuel my life and my work.

—*Maribeth Abrams*

Thank you to Maribeth Abrams for inviting me to join this fun project. I have the deepest appreciation for my parents, H. Jay Dinshah and Freya Dinshah, who raised me as a vegan and encouraged me to be creative with food. They showed me how to have the courage to pursue meaningful employment and true richness in life. I also give special thanks to my vegan roommate, Joe Pipia, for his patience and humor and for sharing his kitchen.

—*Anne Dinshah*

PREFACE: *Why Vegan?*

People avoid eating foods that come from animals for a variety of reasons, including environmental concerns, reverence for life, and health. While a vegan diet may seem limiting, the plant kingdom offers such a vast, colorful array of vegetables, fruits, whole grains, and legumes that vegan diets can be spectacular in terms of variety and flavor. According to the Physicians Committee for Responsible Medicine, a vegan diet (a vegetarian diet that contains no animal foods whatsoever, including no eggs or dairy products) is the healthiest of all, contributing to reduced rates of a broad range of health conditions and diseases, including cancer, cardiovascular disease, diabetes, high blood pressure, kidney stones, and osteoporosis.

The main reason a whole-food vegan diet promotes health is because plant-based foods are high in fiber and low in saturated fat and don't contain cholesterol. Conversely, animal-based foods (beef, eggs, fish, milk, poultry, and so forth) are high in saturated fat and cholesterol and contain no fiber at all. This also explains why people who follow a whole-food vegan diet are less likely to be overweight.

In Western culture, most people are taught from an early age that consuming dairy products is necessary to build strong bones. However, modern research shows that loss of calcium from the body plays a more significant role in bone loss and osteoporosis than insufficient calcium intake. According to the Physicians Committee for Responsible Medicine, a diet high in sulfur-containing amino acids may increase loss of calcium from the bones. The foods highest in sulfur-containing amino acids are those that are animal based, including dairy products. Contrary to popular belief, dairy products are far from the best or only sources of dietary calcium. This mineral is abundant in many delicious plant foods, such as almonds, bok choy, collard greens, kale, red beans, sesame seeds, and white beans.

People often wonder if it's possible to get enough protein on a vegan diet. According to the American Dietetic Association, plant foods can provide sufficient protein if people consume enough calories to meet their energy needs. In truth, the more important question is whether it is possible to eat a meat-based diet without getting *too much* protein. Excessive protein intake has been associated with serious health problems, including cancer, kidney disease, kidney stones, and osteoporosis.

Adopting a vegan diet can be a giant step toward improving your health and well-being. It can also be divinely satisfying in terms of the wonderful tastes and textures that plant foods provide. Meat is rarely prepared without ingredients from the plant kingdom to improve its flavor, such as garlic, onions, herbs, and a wide-array of vegetable-based sauces. These same delicious flavorings can be used with plant foods to create endlessly exciting yet familiar flavors.

For detailed information on the health benefits of a whole-food vegan diet, read *The China Study* by T. Colin Campbell or consult the website of the Physicians Committee for Responsible Medicine: www.pcrm.org.

1

Getting Started

The Pleasure of Quick Cuisine

CHAPTER 1: *Getting Started*

The Pleasure of Quick Cuisine

One of my joys is running into past nutrition clients and students from cooking classes. After the usual greetings, they inevitably tell me with delight about which of the recipes I taught them have since become family favorites. Although everyone has different tastes, certain recipes repeatedly pop up in these conversations.

What do these well-loved recipes have in common? Most importantly, they taste fantastic. And, not surprisingly, they are easy to make. But there's a third trait they all share—every single one of them requires very few ingredients.

Just because a recipe is easy to make doesn't mean it calls for very few ingredients. But even when a majority of ingredients are simply herbs and spices or vegetables that are easy to chop, a recipe can still look daunting. The good news is that scrumptious main dishes, salads, soups, side dishes, beverages, and even desserts can be made with very few ingredients—*just four*, to be exact. And when a recipe that tastes great and is easy to prepare also happens to contain four or fewer ingredients, you know it's going to be a winner.

The recipes in this book comprise only four ingredients or fewer, with the exception of water, salt, pepper, and oil or margarine. Indeed, they're so short and sweet that after preparing most of these recipes once or twice, you may find, as many of my cooking students and nutrition clients have, that you've unknowingly committed them to memory.

A Quick Course on How to Enjoy a Meal

Soft music. Candles. No interruptions. Whispered sweet nothings from the one you love. These added touches can transform a basic meal into a relaxing and memorable occasion. While we can't always have the ideal setting, we can still savor every meal as long as one basic requirement is met—we take the time to sit down and enjoy it.

I'm frequently asked whether it's possible for the average person to whip up a vegan meal quickly enough to still have time to enjoy the fruits of his or her labor. The answer is a resounding yes! In fact, there's no reason for a health-promoting meal to take longer to prepare than one that isn't healthful. One valuable trick is to take advantage of shortcut ingredients. Here are some time-saving tips:

• Create great entrées that contain just one kind of fresh vegetable—ideally broccoli, kale, or another dark leafy green.

• Reach for frozen vegetables, such as artichoke hearts, broccoli, corn, green beans, shiitake mushrooms, or spinach, when more than one vegetable is needed in a recipe.

• Garnish dishes generously with slivered almonds, chopped peanuts, or toasted pine nuts to add richness, crunch, and tantalizing flavor.

• Use canned beans, such as black beans, chickpeas, great northern beans, or pinto beans, to add instant heartiness to main dishes, salads, soups, spreads, and stews.

• Swirl nut or seed butters, such as almond butter, cashew butter, peanut butter, or tahini, into sauces, soups, and stews for extra richness.

• Add a burst of flavor with miso, nutritional yeast flakes, or both.

• Enjoy vegan versions of cream cheese, margarine, mayonnaise, sour cream, and even marshmallow crème for traditional textures and flavors. (But do read the ingredient list carefully to ensure the product is healthful.)

• Use creamy store-bought vegan soups, such as broccoli, butternut squash, corn, or mushroom soup, as the basis for hearty casseroles, sauces, soups, and stews.

• Add great flavor fast with high-quality condiments made without corn syrup, including barbecue sauce, ketchup, mustard, relish, marinades, salad dressings, and simmer sauces.

• Melt vegan chocolate chips to provide the heart and soul of amazing desserts.

Stocking Your Kitchen

You'll find it worthwhile to keep an array of vegan ingredients on hand so that you can make quick and satisfying dishes with very little effort. Keep your kitchen stocked with the basic ingredients described in this section, most of them are readily available at your local supermarket, and you'll be able to put together many of the recipes in this book at a moment's notice. To safeguard your own health as well as the health of your family, friends, and the planet, I recommend that you purchase organic products whenever possible.

Agave nectar. A delicious, low-glycemic liquid sweetener, agave nectar is ideal for use in baked goods or adding to smoothies and sweet sauces. It is readily available in most well-stocked supermarkets and natural food stores in the baking aisle.

Brown rice. Sold in bulk bins at natural food stores or in packages at supermarkets, brown rice has a chewy texture and is more nutritious than white rice. Purchasing an inexpensive rice cooker makes the preparation of brown rice especially easy. For variety, alternate between long-grain brown rice, short-grain brown rice, and brown basmati rice, or stock up on all three.

Canned beans. Peruse the natural food section or the beans and rice aisle of your local supermarket for canned beans, and be sure to read labels carefully. Keep a good variety of organic canned beans on hand, especially black beans, chickpeas (also called garbanzo beans), great northern beans or other white beans, and pinto beans.

Canned tomatoes and tomato products. Look for organic brands of all types of canned tomato products: crushed, diced, and whole tomatoes; paste; and sauce. Try specialty products, such as fire-roasted tomatoes, for unique flavor. Most well-stocked stores also carry canned tomatoes with various seasonings such as garlic, hot chiles, or onions already added.

Condiments. Sometimes everyday condiments are all you need to give a recipe that certain taste. When it comes to standards like balsamic vinegar, barbecue sauce, brown rice vinegar, extra-virgin olive oil, ketchup, mustard, pickle relish, and toasted sesame oil, organic is best. Not only are organic products more healthful, they're often much more flavorful, which is especially important when you're cooking with just a few ingredients.

Dried lentils. At natural food stores, you'll generally find brown lentils in bulk bins. At supermarkets, look in the natural food section or the beans and rice aisle. Brown lentils cook relatively quickly and add flavor, nutrition, and a pleasant texture to many dishes.

Frozen vegetables and fruits. Keep your freezer stocked with frozen vegetables, especially broccoli, corn, green beans, peas, spinach, and vegetable medleys, and fruits, such as blueberries, mixed berries, peaches, and strawberries.

Maple syrup. Most commercial maple syrups are nothing more than sugar, water, maple flavoring, and caramel coloring. Look for real maple syrup, with no additives of any kind, at your natural food store, supermarket, or farmers' market.

Miso. If you've ever had miso soup, you know how rich and flavorful miso is. This nourishing, salty paste made from fermented beans (usually soybeans but other beans too) ranges in color from light, which is sweet and delicate, to dark, which is hearty and saltier. Stored in the refrigerator, miso will keep for a year or longer, but after you indulge in Butternut Sauce (page 67), Cashew "Cheese" Sauce (page 66), or Purple Cabbage with Sesame Sauce (page 105), you may find that you run out of miso much sooner.

Nonstick cooking spray. For cutting down on added fat and making clean-up a breeze, nonstick cooking spray is indispensible. Look for brands that contain organic oils and lecithin.

Nut and seed butters. Choose nut and seed butters that contain only ground nuts or seeds and nothing else, except perhaps salt. Almond butter, cashew butter, peanut butter, tahini, and other nut and seed butters add creamy richness to pasta dishes, soups, spreads, and more. When natural nut and seed butters are stored at room temperature, the oil tends to rise to the surface, so stir them well before using. To keep them fresh, store nut and seed butters in the refrigerator. This will also help keep the oil from separating out.

Nuts and seeds. Raw, unsalted almonds, cashews, peanuts, sesame seeds, and walnuts can be found in the bulk bins at natural food stores and even some well-stocked supermarkets. Scoop up a bagful of each, transfer them to jars at home, and store them in your refrigerator to ensure optimum freshness. Nuts and seeds will keep for about three months in the refrigerator. To double the storage time, transfer them to zipper-lock plastic bags and store them in the freezer.

Nutritional yeast flakes. Not to be confused with brewer's yeast, nutritional yeast, commonly sold in bulk bins at natural food stores, gives nondairy foods a cheesy flavor. These yellow flakes are also a great source of B vitamins. Once you try recipes like Cashew "Cheese" Sauce (page 66) or White Bean Nacho Dip (page 53), you'll be hooked on this delicious ingredient.

Packaged vegetable broth and creamy vegan soups. Several organic brands of vegetable broth and creamy vegan soups are available in aseptic cartons in both natural food stores and the natural food section of supermarkets. These flavorful products are versatile and extremely handy for putting together quick stews and casseroles, such as Almost-Instant Minestrone (page 37), Broccoli-Rice Casserole (page 115), and Creamy Millet Casserole (page 118). Stock your pantry with a carton of vegetable broth and several creamy vegan soups, especially broccoli, butternut squash, corn, and mushroom soup.

Salsa. There are many different types of jarred salsa available, from mild and tangy to super-hot and spicy. Look for brands made with organic tomatoes and that have a heat level you can tolerate.

Spaghetti sauce. There are so many different kinds of vegan spaghetti sauce available that you are certain to find several you like. Look for organic brands in jars rather than cans (to avoid the transfer of any metallic taste).

Tempeh. A fermented food made from whole soybeans, sometimes in combination with grains or other ingredients, tempeh is high in protein and fiber. It is stocked in the refrigerated section of natural food stores, usually near the tofu, and comes in a thin, firm block. Tempeh can also be stored in the freezer, so pick some up the next time you go shopping. That way you'll have it on hand if you spontaneously decide to whip up some Barbecue Tempeh (page 89) or Tempeh "Chicken" Salad (page 49).

Tofu. Regular tofu is packed in water in plastic tubs and sold in the refrigerated section of supermarkets and natural food stores. It comes in different densities (soft, firm, and extra-firm), and it's best to buy the kind that a recipe calls for. Silken tofu, which is much softer and creamier than regular tofu, usually comes in an aseptic box and is found on the grocery shelves rather than in the refrigerated section. As with water-packed tofu, it's best to purchase the kind of silken tofu called for in a recipe. Although silken tofu has a longer shelf life than regular tofu, you still need to keep an eye on the expiration date.

Vegan cheese. For the recipes in this book, purchase vegan cheeses known for their good flavor and ability to melt. There are a number of different brands on the market, so try several until you find the ones you like best.

Vegan mayonnaise. Unlike traditional mayonnaise, vegan mayonnaise doesn't include egg products. At natural food stores you'll find a many different brands, mostly in the condiment aisle, and at least one excellent brand in the refrigerated section. Try different ones to see which you like best. Most large supermarkets carry at least one brand of vegan mayonnaise in the natural food section.

Vegan sausage. Vegan sausage adds great texture and satisfying flavor to many quick dishes. Look for it in the refrigerated section (near the tofu) of your natural food store or supermarket.

Vegan sour cream. Vegan sour cream is an important ingredient in certain dips and adds the finishing touch to south-of-the-border fare like Black Bean Roll-Ups (page 83). Before purchasing vegan sour cream, check the label to make sure it doesn't contain hydrogenated fat.

Morning Meals

CHAPTER 2: *Morning Meals*

Sweet-and-Creamy Hot Rice Cereal

YIELD: *3 to 4 servings*

Rice cereal, or rice pudding, sounds like an old-fashioned dish, and it seems that people don't gravitate toward it much these days. I challenge the trend! Nourishing for the body and nurturing for the soul, this hot and creamy cereal is so good that I'm happy to eat it any time of day. This recipe starts with uncooked rice, but you can save time by preparing the rice the night before or by using about three cups of leftover rice.

2 cups water
1 cup short-grain brown rice
¾ cup vanilla nondairy milk
⅓ cup dried cherries or other dried fruit (chopped, if necessary)
2 to 4 tablespoons maple syrup

Combine the water and rice in a small, heavy saucepan. Bring to a boil over medium-high heat. Turn the heat down to low, cover, and cook for about 45 minutes, or until the water is absorbed.

Stir in the nondairy milk and cherries. Stir in the maple syrup to taste. Increase the heat to medium-high and bring to a boil. Turn the heat down to low and cook, stirring occasionally, for 5 to 10 minutes, or until the desired thickness is achieved. Serve immediately.

Per serving: calories: 234, protein: 5 g, fat: 2 g, carbohydrate: 47 g, fiber: 3 g, sodium: 22 mg

Cream of Quinoa: Replace the rice with 1 cup of quinoa (rinsed well) and decrease the initial cooking time to about 15 minutes, or until the water is absorbed.

Tip: It's a good idea to rinse quinoa before using it, as quinoa has a naturally occurring coating that can be bitter. Simply put the measured, uncooked quinoa in a large bowl and fill it with water. The quinoa will sink to the bottom of the bowl. Swish the quinoa around with your hands for about 5 seconds; then pour off the water. Repeat this process; then drain through a fine-mesh sieve. The quinoa is now clean and ready to use.

Cashew French Toast

YIELD: *about 11 slices*

Making perfect vegan french toast is an art that requires a fair amount of intuition. It's important to be patient and resist the urge to flip the bread too soon. You will be richly rewarded with absolutely phenomenal french toast. How good? Don't be surprised if you go through an entire loaf of bread in one morning, with people still clamoring for more. Needless to say, it's delicious topped with maple syrup.

1¼ cups vanilla nondairy milk
¾ cup raw cashews
¼ cup quick-cooking oats
Optional: ½ teaspoon ground cinnamon
Nonhydrogenated vegan margarine
About 11 slices whole-grain bread

Combine the nondairy milk, cashews, and oats in a blender. Add the cinnamon, if using. Process until completely smooth. Pour the mixture into an 8-inch square baking pan or a flat-bottomed bowl of similar size.

Place a covered casserole dish in the oven and preheat the oven to warm.

Heat about 2 teaspoons of margarine in a nonstick skillet or heavy griddle over medium heat. When it starts to sizzle, dip a slice of the bread into the cashew mixture. Let any excess drip back into the pan or bowl. Place the dipped bread in the skillet. Repeat with 1 or 2 more slices of bread—however many can fit in the skillet without touching.

Cook for 5 to 7 minutes on the first side, or until the tops start to look a bit dry. Gently flip the slices over and cook the other side for about 5 minutes, or until golden brown. Transfer to the casserole dish and cover to keep warm. Repeat with the remaining batter and bread.

Per slice: calories: 165, protein: 5 g, fat: 6 g, carbohydrate: 24 g, fiber: 1 g, sodium: 181 mg

Tip: To freeze leftover french toast, arrange the prepared pieces in a single layer on a baking sheet. Place in the freezer for 2 to 3 hours. Transfer the frozen french toast to a freezer-safe container or zipper-lock freezer bag. Store in the freezer for up to 3 weeks.

Unused batter can be refrigerated for 2 days; however, it may thicken when chilled. If necessary, stir in a small amount of water or nondairy milk, 1 tablespoon at a time, to achieve the desired consistency.

Buckwheat Pancakes

YIELD: *about 10 pancakes*

Having a reliable vegan pancake recipe is invaluable, and this one fits the bill. This recipe uses a high proportion of buckwheat, a nutty-flavored flour ground from the starchy seeds of a plant in the dock family. It is reputed to help lower high cholesterol and regulate blood pressure. Serve these delicious pancakes with pure maple syrup, fruit-sweetened jam, or Peach Sauce (page 140).

1½ cups buckwheat flour
1 cup whole wheat flour
1 tablespoon baking powder
3¼ cups nondairy milk (plain or vanilla)
2 tablespoons vegetable oil

Put the buckwheat flour, whole wheat flour, and baking powder in a large mixing bowl. Whisk to combine. Add the nondairy milk and vegetable oil. Stir just until combined.

Lightly mist a large nonstick skillet or heavy griddle with nonstick cooking spray and place it over medium heat. When a drop of water added to the skillet sizzles, the skillet is hot enough to cook the pancakes. Use a ½-cup measuring cup to portion the batter into the skillet, fitting as many pancakes as you can while keeping a bit of space between them. Cook for about 5 minutes, until bubbles appear on the tops. Gently flip the pancakes over. Cook the other side for about 5 minutes, or until golden brown. Place the cooked pancakes on a serving platter and cover them with foil or a clean dish towel to keep them warm while you cook the remaining batter. Continue this process until all the batter has been used, misting the skillet with additional nonstick cooking spray between each batch as needed. Serve immediately.

Per pancake: calories: 168, protein: 7 g, fat: 5 g, carbohydrate: 23 g, fiber: 3 g, sodium: 144 mg

Blueberry-Buckwheat Pancakes: Stir 1 cup of fresh blueberries or thawed frozen blueberries into the batter.

Chocolate Chip Pancakes: Stir 1 cup of vegan chocolate chips into the batter.

Strawberry-Banana Gel

YIELD: *8 servings*

This colorful fruit concoction will give you plenty of energy to start your day. Just be aware that you need to plan ahead, as it must be made the night before. This fruity gel also makes a delicious dessert.

4 cups pineapple juice
6 tablespoons quick-cooking tapioca
1 pound fresh strawberries, hulled and chopped
2 bananas, chopped

Combine the juice and tapioca in a large saucepan over medium-high heat. Bring to a boil, stirring frequently. Remove from the heat and set aside to cool for 10 minutes.

Put the strawberries and bananas in a large serving bowl with a diameter of about 9 inches. Stir gently. Pour the cooled juice mixture over the fruit. The fruit should be immersed in the liquid, but it's okay if some of it floats to the top. Refrigerate for 8 to 12 hours, or until the gel is set. Serve chilled.

Per serving: calories: 131, protein: 1 g, fat: 0.3 g, carbohydrate: 30 g, fiber: 2 g, sodium: 2 mg

Zippy Potatoes O'Brien

YIELD: *4 to 6 servings*

Red bell pepper lends a delicate sweetness to these chunky potatoes, and onion and zippy salsa bring it all together for awesome taste and texture. This dish is hearty enough to stand on its own, or serve it as a side dish or part of a special brunch.

3 large white potatoes, scrubbed and cut into ½-inch chunks
1 cup salsa
4 teaspoons extra-virgin olive oil
Salt and ground black pepper
1 onion, chopped
1 red bell pepper, chopped
Optional: chopped green onions

Preheat the oven to 375 degrees F. Lightly mist a baking sheet with nonstick cooking spray.

Combine the potatoes, ½ cup of the salsa, and 2 teaspoons of the oil in a large bowl. Sprinkle generously with salt and pepper. Stir until the potatoes are evenly coated. Spread the potatoes in a single layer on the prepared baking sheet. Roast for 30 minutes, or until tender.

Heat the remaining 2 teaspoons of oil in a large nonstick skillet over medium-high heat (see tip). Add the onion and cook and stir for about 10 minutes, or until browned. Add the bell pepper and cook and stir for 5 minutes. Add the potatoes and cook and stir for 5 to 7 minutes, or until browned. Stir in the remaining ½ cup of salsa. Cook, stirring occasionally, for about 5 more minutes, or until hot and bubbly. Season with salt and pepper to taste. Garnish with chopped green onions, if desired.

Per serving: calories: 176, protein: 4 g, fat: 4 g, carbohydrate: 31 g, fiber: 4 g, sodium: 253 mg

Tip: If you don't use a nonstick pan, be sure to use a heavy skillet. If the potatoes start to stick, add water, 1 tablespoon at a time, just until they don't stick.

Baked Bean and Tater Casserole

YIELD: *4 servings*

This is a satisfying casserole to fuel a brisk winter morning adventure. You'll be ready for action after loading up on such hearty fare.

30 frozen store-bought potato nuggets (such as Tater Tots)
2 cups chopped vegetables (see tip)
1 can (14 ounces) vegan baked beans

Preheat the oven to 375 degrees F.

Arrange the potato nuggets over the bottom of an 8-inch square baking pan. Layer the vegetables over the potatoes. Spread the baked beans over the vegetables.

Bake for 20 to 30 minutes, or until the vegetables are tender and the liquid from the baked beans has thickened slightly. Serve immediately.

Per serving: calories: 231, protein: 8 g, fat: 5 g, carbohydrate: 37 g, fiber: 7 g, sodium: 658 mg

Tip: When choosing the vegetables, use all quick-cooking vegetables, such as bell peppers, corn, mushrooms, spinach, tomatoes, and zucchini. Alternatively, use only shredded slower-cooking vegetables, such as beets, butternut squash, and carrots. This ensures that all of the vegetables will be cooked to the same tenderness.

Tater Casserole with Hummus: Use 2 cups of hummus in place of the baked beans, and sprinkle the top of the casserole with 1 teaspoon of paprika. Bake for 20 to 30 minutes, or until the vegetables are tender and the hummus is golden but not browned.

Morning Muffin Sandwich

YIELD: *3 servings*

With a mainstream flavor that even nonvegans adore, this breakfast sandwich makes for a hot and filling meal with a minimum of preparation time. It's a great way to introduce tofu to people who haven't had it before, because it tastes surprisingly like a fried egg sandwich.

1 container (1 pound) extra-firm regular tofu, rinsed, drained, and patted dry
2 tablespoons nonhydrogenated vegan margarine
2 tablespoons nutritional yeast flakes
Salt and ground black pepper
2 cups frozen spinach (defrosted), or 3 cups fresh spinach
3 English muffins, split in half

Slice the tofu widthwise into 9 rectangles, each about ½ inch wide. Melt 1 tablespoon of the margarine in a nonstick or heavy skillet over medium-high heat. When the margarine starts to sizzle, arrange the tofu slices in a single layer in the skillet (if your skillet is small, you may need to cook the tofu in batches). Sprinkle with 1 tablespoon of the nutritional yeast and season with salt and pepper to taste. Cook for 7 minutes. Gently flip the tofu over. Sprinkle with the remaining tablespoon of nutritional yeast and salt and pepper to taste. Cook the second side for about 7 minutes, or until golden brown. Transfer the cooked tofu to a small baking dish. Cover to keep warm and set aside. Do not turn the heat off under the skillet.

Add the spinach to the hot skillet and cook, stirring frequently, for 2 to 4 minutes, or until hot and tender.

Toast the English muffin halves. Spread the remaining tablespoon of margarine on the muffins. Arrange the fried tofu on the bottom halves of the muffins. Top with the cooked spinach and remaining English muffin halves. Serve immediately.

Per serving: calories: 386, protein: 29 g, fat: 15 g, carbohydrate: 31 g, fiber: 8 g, sodium: 393 mg

3

Beverages

CHAPTER 3: *Beverages*

Banana-Nut Smoothie

YIELD: *2 servings*

This sophisticated and mildly sweet smoothie tastes great and is also loaded with fiber.

½ cup blanched almonds, slivered almonds, or raw cashews
1¾ cups vanilla nondairy milk
1 frozen banana
¼ teaspoon ground cinnamon
Optional: pinch ground nutmeg

Combine the almonds and ½ cup of the nondairy milk in a blender. Process until completely smooth. Add the remaining 1¼ cups of nondairy milk, the frozen banana, and the cinnamon. Process until smooth. Garnish with the ground nutmeg, if desired. Serve immediately.

Per serving: calories: 402, protein: 14 g, fat: 22 g, carbohydrate: 35 g, fiber: 5 g, sodium: 90 mg

Luscious Strawberry Frappé

YIELD: *2 servings*

This heavenly frappé (also known as a milkshake) is so delicate in flavor and creamy in texture that no added sweetener is needed.

⅔ cup raw cashews
1⅓ cups vanilla nondairy milk
1 frozen banana
1 cup frozen strawberries

Combine the cashews and ⅔ cup of the nondairy milk in a blender. Process until completely smooth, adding a bit more milk if necessary to make a smooth cream with absolutely no crunchy bits remaining. Add the remaining nondairy milk, the banana, and the strawberries. Process until smooth. Serve immediately.

Per serving: calories: 423, protein: 13 g, fat: 22 g, carbohydrate: 43 g, fiber: 4 g, sodium: 67 mg

Cherry Kiss

YIELD: *2 servings*

Chocolate and cherries come together to create a beverage that's both luscious and high in antioxidants. Because it contains frozen banana, this could be considered a smoothie, so you could even enjoy it for breakfast for a special treat.

1½ cups vanilla nondairy milk
1 frozen banana
⅔ cup frozen cherries
1 tablespoon unsweetened cocoa powder

Combine all of the ingredients in a blender. Process until smooth. Serve immediately.

Per serving: calories: 195, protein: 6 g, fat: 3 g, carbohydrate: 35 g, fiber: 3 g, sodium: 70 mg

Mellow Mango-Peach Smoothie

YIELD: *2 servings*

Utterly refreshing and subtly sweet, this smoothie pairs mangoes and peaches with almonds and nutmeg for sophisticated flair.

1½ cups vanilla almond milk or other nondairy milk
1 cup frozen peaches
1 cup frozen mango chunks
Pinch ground nutmeg

Combine all of the ingredients in a blender. Process until completely smooth. Serve immediately.

Per serving: calories: 199, protein: 6 g, fat: 3 g, carbohydrate: 37 g, fiber: 3 g, sodium: 69 mg

Strawberry Colada

YIELD: *2 servings*

Coconut and pineapple are a classic combination in this well-loved Caribbean quaff, and strawberries only add to the appeal. Feel free to add some rum if you like.

2¾ cups coconut juice blend (see tip)
⅔ cup frozen pineapple chunks
⅔ cup frozen strawberries

Combine all of the ingredients in a blender. Process until smooth. Serve immediately.

Per serving: calories: 263, protein: 1 g, fat: 22 g, carbohydrate: 16 g, fiber: 2 g, sodium: 2 mg

Tip: Coconut juice blends, typically containing coconut milk and white grape juice, can be found in the natural food section of large supermarkets and in the juice aisle at natural food stores. If you can't find something like this, use pure coconut milk instead. It will be thicker and more filling, and still very delicious.

Kale Chill

YIELD: *2 servings*

With their powerful and bright flavors, pineapple and raspberries effectively conceal the bitterness of kale, making it possible to drink healthful fresh greens in a sweet and frosty concoction.

1½ cups vanilla nondairy milk
1 cup frozen pineapple chunks, frozen raspberries, or a combination
½ cup chopped kale (1 to 2 leaves)
1 tablespoon agave nectar

Combine all of the ingredients in a blender. Process until completely smooth. Serve immediately.

Per serving: calories: 189, protein: 5 g, fat: 2 g, carbohydrate: 36 g, fiber: 1 g, sodium: 75 mg

Frozen Strawberry Lemonade

YIELD: *2 servings*

Agave nectar makes a great stand-in for granulated sweetener in this heat-busting summertime treat.

½ cup agave nectar
½ cup freshly squeezed lemon juice (2 to 3 lemons)
1½ cups water
1 cup frozen strawberries

Combine all of the ingredients in a blender. Process until completely smooth. Serve immediately.

Per serving: calories: 281, protein: 1 g, fat: 0 g, carbohydrate: 74 g, fiber: 2 g, sodium: 20 mg

Raspberry-Lime Cooler
YIELD: *2 servings*

This cooler is not too tart, not too sweet, and absolutely gorgeous in color. Make a big batch for your next backyard party and serve it in a glass pitcher to show it off.

1 cup frozen raspberries
½ cup agave nectar
½ cup freshly squeezed lime juice (about 5 limes)
1 cup club soda

Combine the raspberries, agave nectar, and lime juice in a blender. Process until completely smooth. Pour the mixture into glasses or a pitcher. Add the club soda and stir gently to combine. Serve immediately.

Per serving: calories: 333, protein: 0 g, fat: 1 g, carbohydrate: 81 g, fiber: 6 g, sodium: 26 mg

Champagne Cooler: Replace the club soda with champagne or another sparkling wine.

Peanut Butter Cup

YIELD: *2 servings*

My daughter Ivy is crazy about this shake. A true chocolate princess, she carefully maneuvers her straw over the garnish of drizzled chocolate sauce and sucks it up before it has a chance to soak into the nutty, frozen concoction.

1½ cups vanilla nondairy milk
3 generous scoops vegan chocolate ice cream
⅓ cup smooth unsalted peanut butter
Optional: vegan chocolate sauce

Combine the nondairy milk, vegan ice cream, and peanut butter in a blender. Process until smooth. Serve immediately, garnished with a swirl of chocolate sauce, if desired.

Per serving: calories: 540, protein: 19 g, fat: 32 g, carbohydrate: 44 g, fiber: 5 g, sodium: 165 mg

Almond Butter Cup: Replace the peanut butter with almond butter.

4

Soups

CHAPTER 4: *Soups*

Red Onion Soup

YIELD: *4 servings*

This soup is divine in its simplicity. Patience is the key, both when caramelizing the onions and during their long, slow simmering in vegetable broth.

5 red onions, chopped
3 tablespoons extra-virgin olive oil
¼ teaspoon organic sugar
5 cups vegetable broth
3 bay leaves

Put the onions in a large, heavy soup pot, pour in the oil, and toss until evenly coated. Cook and stir over medium-high heat for 15 minutes. Stir in the sugar. Cook and stir for an additional 15 to 20 minutes, or until the onions are soft and brown.

Stir in the vegetable broth and bay leaves. Increase the heat to high and bring to a boil. Turn the heat down to low, cover, and cook, stirring occasionally, for 1 hour. Remove the bay leaves or let them float for decoration (just don't eat them).

Per serving: calories: 180, protein: 2 g, fat: 10 g, carbohydrate: 17 g, fiber: 5 g, sodium: 107 mg

Tips: Leftover cooking water from Harvest Mash (page 108) can be used as the broth in this soup.

Great Greens Soup

YIELD: *4 to 6 servings*

This is a great soup for those who love greens, but even people who are finicky about vegetables find it delicious.

5 cups water
3 small heads bok choy, chopped
2 potatoes, scrubbed and chopped
¼ head cabbage, chopped
1 pound frozen peas, thawed
Salt and ground black pepper

Combine the water, bok choy, potatoes, and cabbage in a heavy soup pot over high heat. Bring to a boil. Turn the heat down to low, cover, and cook, stirring occasionally, for about 20 minutes, or until the potatoes are tender.

Remove from the heat. Process until smooth using a handheld blender. Alternatively, cool the soup until it's barely steaming; then process it until smooth in batches in a standard blender and return it to the pot. (Don't fill the blender more than one-third full during processing, or the steam could force off the lid.) Stir in the peas. Reheat as needed. Season with salt and pepper to taste before serving.

Per serving: calories: 36, protein: 2 g, fat: 0 g, carbohydrate: 6 g, fiber: 2 g, sodium: 16 mg

Pumpkin-Bean Soup

YIELD: *4 servings*

This creamy soup provides a delightful introduction to a hearty meal on a chilly autumn day. And it couldn't be easier to make. Once all of the ingredients are combined in a pot, they require just a brief time to cook. No need to bring the soup to a boil—just heat it to whatever temperature you like.

1 can (28 ounces) pumpkin purée
3 cups unsweetened nondairy milk
1 teaspoon ground ginger
1 can (14.5 ounces) white beans (such as cannellini or great northern beans), rinsed and drained
Salt and ground black pepper

Combine the pumpkin, nondairy milk, and ginger in a large, heavy saucepan. Stir in the beans. Cook over medium heat for about 5 minutes, or until the soup reaches the desired serving temperature. Season with salt and pepper to taste. Serve immediately.

Per serving: calories: 282, protein: 17 g, fat: 4 g, carbohydrate: 37 g, fiber: 11 g, sodium: 94 mg

Sweet-and-Sour Cabbage Soup

YIELD: *6 to 8 servings*

Although this version of the traditional Russian dish is made with two very unusual ingredients—ginger ale and ketchup—it has a surprisingly authentic flavor. For optimal flavor, choose an organic ketchup free of corn syrup and white sugar, and splurge on a high-quality soda, preferably sweetened with fruit juice.

36 ounces ginger ale
1¾ cups (14 ounces) ketchup
1 medium to large head green cabbage, shredded
Salt and ground black pepper

Combine the ginger ale and ketchup in a heavy soup pot and mix well. Stir in the cabbage. Bring to a boil over high heat. Cook, stirring frequently, for 3 to 5 minutes. Turn the heat down to low, cover, and cook, stirring occasionally, for about 1 hour, or until the cabbage is very tender. Season with salt and pepper to taste before serving.

Per serving: calories: 145, protein: 2 g, fat: 0 g, carbohydrate: 33 g, fiber: 4 g, sodium: 792 mg

Sweet-and-Sour Cabbage and Potato Soup: Add 1 potato, peeled and cut into 3/4-inch chunks, when you stir in the cabbage.

Artichoke, Leek, and White Bean Soup

YIELD: *8 servings*

The smooth texture and creamy richness of this fiber-packed soup provide the perfect backdrop for its sophisticated flavors. Look for frozen artichoke hearts at your local supermarket; although they can be hard to find, they are significantly higher in flavor than canned artichoke hearts, and superior in texture and overall quality too.

1 tablespoon extra-virgin olive oil
3 leeks, white parts only, chopped and washed (see tip)
2 packages (9 ounces each) frozen artichoke hearts, thawed
1 carton (32 ounces) vegetable broth
2 cans (15.5 ounces each) great northern beans or other white beans,
    rinsed and drained
Salt and ground black pepper
Optional: lemon wedges

Heat the oil in a heavy soup pot over medium-high heat. Add the leeks and cook and stir for about 7 minutes, or until the leeks are tender and golden brown. Add the artichoke hearts and cook and stir for 5 minutes. Stir in the vegetable broth. Bring to a boil. Turn the heat down to low, cover, and cook for 20 minutes, stirring occasionally. Stir in the beans. Cook for 10 minutes longer.

Remove from the heat. Process until smooth using a handheld blender. Alternatively, cool the soup until it's barely steaming; then process it until smooth in batches in a standard blender and return it to the pot. (Don't fill the blender more than one-third full during processing, or the steam could force off the lid.) Season with salt and pepper to taste. Garnish each serving with a lemon wedge, if desired.

Per serving: calories: 184, protein: 10 g, fat: 1 g, carbohydrate: 28 g, fiber: 9 g, sodium: 142 mg

Tip: To prepare the leeks, cut off the root ends and the greens. Discard the roots and, if you like, save the greens for use in another recipe. Chop the white parts; then transfer them to a colander. Rinse them thoroughly under running water. Drain well before using.

Ginger-Kissed Butternut Squash Soup

YIELD: *4 servings*

Although delicious on its own, store-bought creamy vegan butternut squash soup reaches a new height in flavor when enhanced with peanut butter, fresh ginger, and a pinch of cayenne.

1 carton (32 ounces) creamy vegan butternut squash soup
1 tablespoon smooth unsalted peanut butter
2 teaspoons grated fresh ginger
Pinch cayenne

Put all of the ingredients in a large, heavy saucepan over medium-high heat. Whisk until thoroughly combined. Bring to a simmer. Turn the heat down to low, cover, and cook for 20 minutes, stirring occasionally.

Per serving: calories: 102, protein: 3 g, fat: 4 g, carbohydrate: 15 g, fiber: 1 g, sodium: 484 mg

Almost-Instant Minestrone

YIELD: *8 servings*

A wide variety of smooth and creamy vegan soups are available in quart-size, shelf-stable packages. They provide a foolproof base for thick and chunky cold-weather soups such as this one, filled with beans, vegetables, and pasta.

1 tablespoon extra-virgin olive oil
3 cups bite-size mixed vegetables (such as broccoli, corn, green beans, kale, mushrooms, or peas)
1 carton (32 ounces) creamy vegan tomato soup
6 ounces elbow macaroni or rotini
1 can (15 ounces) kidney beans, rinsed and drained
Salt and ground black pepper

Heat the oil in a heavy soup pot over medium-high heat. Add the vegetables and cook and stir for about 10 minutes, or until softened. Stir in the tomato soup and bring to a simmer. Turn the heat down to low, cover, and cook for 20 minutes.

Meanwhile, cook the macaroni in a large pot of boiling water until almost tender. Drain the macaroni and stir it into the soup. Stir in the beans. Cover and cook for 10 minutes. Season with salt and pepper to taste before serving.

Per serving: calories: 151, protein: 8 g, fat: 1 g, carbohydrate: 24 g, fiber: 5 g, sodium: 243 mg

Thai Vegetable Soup

YIELD: *8 servings*

It's easy to turn store-bought creamy vegan butternut squash soup into fantastic Thai-inspired fare with just a few simple additions: coconut milk, fresh or frozen vegetables, and fresh basil. Just check the natural food section at large supermarkets or the soup aisle at natural food stores for creamy vegan butternut squash soup in a one-quart carton.

1 carton (32 ounces) creamy vegan butternut squash soup
1 can (14 ounces) coconut milk
3 cups bite-size mixed fresh vegetables, or 1 package (16 ounces) frozen mixed Chinese vegetables, thawed and drained well
3 to 4 tablespoons chopped fresh basil

Combine the butternut squash soup and coconut milk in a heavy soup pot and mix well. Bring to a boil over medium-high heat. Stir in the vegetables. Turn the heat down to low, cover, and simmer for about 20 minutes, or until the vegetables are tender. Stir in the basil just before serving.

Per serving: calories: 143, protein: 2 g, fat: 11 g, carbohydrate: 8 g, fiber: 2 g, sodium: 249 mg

Thai Curry Vegetable Soup: Add 1 to 2 teaspoons of curry powder to the soup along with the vegetables.

Tomato-Rice Soup

YIELD: *8 servings*

Store-bought creamy vegan tomato soup is the perfect base for a wide variety of soups. Here, it's rounded out with assorted vegetables, cooked rice, and a bit of broth. And not only is this soup easy, it's also hearty, filling, and rich in fiber.

4 cups vegetable broth
1 cup brown rice
1 carton (32 ounces) creamy vegan tomato soup
4 - 5 cups bite-size mixed vegetables (such as broccoli, cauliflower, corn, onion, peas, red bell pepper, yellow squash, or zucchini)
Salt and ground black pepper

Pour 2 cups of the vegetable broth into a small, heavy saucepan. Add the rice. Bring to a boil over medium-high heat. Turn the heat down to low, cover, and cook for about 45 minutes, or until the broth is absorbed and the rice is tender.

    While the rice is cooking, combine the tomato soup and the remaining 2 cups of vegetable broth in a heavy soup pot and mix well. Bring to a boil over medium-high heat. Stir in the vegetables. Turn the heat down to low, cover, and cook for about 30 minutes, or until the vegetables are tender. Stir in the cooked rice. Season with salt and pepper to taste before serving.

Per serving: calories: 98, protein: 4 g, fat: 1 g, carbohydrate: 18 g, fiber: 3 g, sodium: 368 mg

5

Salads

CHAPTER 5: *Salads*

Roasted Beet Salad with Raspberry Vinaigrette

YIELD: *4 servings*

Roasted beets are accompanied by baby lettuce and walnuts in this gorgeous, sophisticated salad. For optimal flavor, choose a high-quality organic raspberry vinaigrette.

4 beets (peeled or unpeeled), cut into ¾-inch chunks (about 4 cups)
1 tablespoon extra-virgin olive oil
4 cups mixed baby lettuce or spring mix
½ cup chopped walnuts, toasted (see tip)
¼ to ⅓ cup raspberry vinaigrette
Salt and ground black pepper

Preheat the oven to 400 degrees F. Mist a baking sheet with nonstick cooking spray.

Put the beets in a large bowl. Drizzle with the oil and toss to coat. Arrange the beets in a single layer on the prepared pan. Roast for about 50 minutes, or until tender. Set aside to cool.

Put the beets, lettuce, and walnuts in a large salad bowl. Drizzle the vinaigrette over the beet mixture. Toss gently to combine. Season with salt and pepper to taste. Serve immediately.

Per serving: calories: 184, protein: 4 g, fat: 13 g, carbohydrate: 12 g, fiber: 3 g, sodium: 143 mg

Tip: To toast walnuts, put them in a dry skillet over medium-high heat. Cook, stirring constantly, for about 3 minutes, or until fragrant and slightly darkened.

Potato Salad Americana

YIELD: *8 servings*

This is my take on the classic, all-American potato salad. Serve it at any gathering and watch it disappear.

4 large potatoes, peeled and cut into large chunks
¾ cup vegan mayonnaise
½ cup vegan sour cream
4 green onions, finely chopped, or ¼ cup finely chopped red onion
Salt and ground black pepper
Optional: 1 tablespoon chopped fresh parsley

Fill a large saucepan halfway with water and bring to a boil over high heat. Add the potatoes and cook for about 10 to 15 minutes, or until fork-tender. Drain the potatoes and let them cool.

Cut the potatoes into bite-size chunks. Put them in a large bowl. Add the vegan mayonnaise, vegan sour cream, and green onions. Stir gently to combine. Season with salt and pepper to taste. Gently stir in the parsley, if desired. Refrigerate for at least 2 hours before serving.

Per serving: calories: 220, protein: 2 g, fat: 13 g, carbohydrate: 23 g, fiber: 2 g, sodium: 95 mg

Wild Rice Salad

YIELD: *4 servings*

In this recipe, combining a multicolored rice blend with marinated artichoke hearts and red bell peppers creates a colorful and deliciously chewy salad. Choose a high-quality organic vinaigrette, as it's the primary source of flavor for the salad.

3 cups water
1½ cups wild rice blend (see tip)
1 jar (6.5 ounces) marinated artichoke hearts, drained
2 red bell peppers, chopped
⅓ to ½ cup red wine and olive oil vinaigrette

Combine the water and rice blend in a small, heavy saucepan. Bring to a boil over medium-high heat. Turn the heat down to low, cover, and cook for about 45 minutes, or until the rice is tender. Transfer to a large mixing bowl. Set aside until completely cool.

Add the artichoke hearts and peppers to the rice. Mix well. Drizzle the vinaigrette over the rice mixture. Stir until everything is evenly coated. Refrigerate for at least 3 hours before serving.

Per serving: calories: 283, protein: 7 g, fat: 12 g, carbohydrate: 33 g, fiber: 4 g, sodium: 142 mg

Tip: Wild rice blends are sold in bulk at natural food stores and in packages in the rice or natural food section of supermarkets.

Very Veggie Rice Salad: Stir in 2 green onions, chopped, and 1 cup of thawed frozen peas.

Fiesta Rice Salad

YIELD: *6 servings*

Rice, beans, and corn go so well together. Here, their flavors are intensified by cilantro salsa, which marries the ingredients, creating a festive and hearty main dish salad.

1¾ cups water
½ cup brown rice
1 cup frozen corn kernels
1 can (15 ounces) black beans, rinsed and drained
1 cup cilantro salsa

Pour 1¼ cups of the water into a small saucepan. Add the rice. Bring to a boil over medium-high heat. Turn the heat down to low, cover, and cook for about 45 minutes, or until the water is absorbed. Transfer to a large bowl. Set aside to cool.

Combine the corn and the remaining ½ cup of water in a small saucepan. Bring to a boil over medium-high heat. Turn the heat down to low, cover, and cook for about 5 minutes, or until the corn is tender. Drain. Add the corn and black beans to the rice. Stir until evenly combined. Let cool to room temperature. Add the salsa just before serving. Stir until all the ingredients are evenly coated.

Per serving: calories: 153, protein: 6 g, fat: 0.5 g, carbohydrate: 30 g, fiber: 6 g, sodium: 151 mg

Tip: If you can't find cilantro salsa, use your favorite salsa plus ⅓ cup of chopped fresh cilantro.

To save time, prepare the rice for this recipe in advance. Alternatively, use 1½ cups of leftover cooked rice.

Succotash Salad

YIELD: *6 servings*

Vibrant with red, green, and yellow vegetables, this appealing light salad makes excellent use of lima beans.

1 pound frozen large lima beans
1 pound frozen corn kernels
1½ cups water
1 red bell pepper, chopped
½ to 1 cup chopped fresh parsley
Salt and ground black pepper

Combine the lima beans, corn, and water in a medium saucepan. Bring to a boil over high heat. Turn the heat down to medium-low and cook for about 10 minutes, or until the lima beans are tender. Drain the vegetables, return them to the saucepan, and cool for 15 minutes.

Stir in the bell pepper and parsley and season with salt and pepper to taste. Serve immediately.

Per serving: calories: 162, protein: 8 g, fat: 0.5 g, carbohydrate: 28 g, fiber: 6 g, sodium: 21 mg

Tip: Using 1 cup of parsley will impart a strong flavor; using ½ cup will provide more of an accent.

Aegean Chickpea Salad

YIELD: *3 servings*

Capers lend an intriguing, salty bite to this colorful salad of chickpeas, roasted red bell peppers, and artichokes. This is excellent as a side dish or picnic fare, or as the basis of a delightful pasta salad, as described in the variation below.

1 can (15.5 ounces) chickpeas, rinsed and drained
1 jar (6.5 ounces) marinated artichoke hearts, drained and chopped
½ cup roasted red bell peppers, chopped (see tip)
2 tablespoons capers, rinsed and drained
1 tablespoon extra-virgin olive oil
Salt and ground black pepper

Combine all of the ingredients in a bowl and mix well. Serve immediately. Alternatively, transfer to a storage container and refrigerate until ready to serve.

Aegean Pasta Salad: Stir 2 tablespoons of vegan mayonnaise into the salad. Cook 8 ounces of elbow macaroni or penne in boiling water until tender. Drain. Add the macaroni to the salad. Stir gently until thoroughly combined. Refrigerate for at least 2 hours before serving.

Per serving: calories: 207, protein: 10 g, fat: 6 g, carbohydrate: 27 g, fiber: 7 g, sodium: 362 mg

Tip: Roasted red bell peppers are available in jars or cans at most supermarkets. You can also roast your own peppers. Directions for doing so are in the Vineyard Peppers recipe, page 61.

Green Bean, Cucumber, and White Bean Salad

YIELD: *8 servings*

Green beans, cucumber, and white beans are tossed with an Asian vinaigrette for a crisp and delicate salad. English cucumbers taste especially good in this recipe.

1 pound frozen cut green beans

1 cup water

1 cucumber, chopped

1 can (15 ounces) white beans (such as cannellini beans or great northern beans), rinsed and drained

¼ cup bottled Asian-flavored vinaigrette

Put the green beans and water in a medium saucepan. Bring to a boil over medium-high heat. Turn the heat down to low and cook for about 5 minutes, or until the beans are tender but still bright green. Drain. Transfer to a large bowl and set aside to cool.

Add the cucumber, white beans, and vinaigrette to the green beans. Stir gently until the vegetables and beans are evenly coated. Serve immediately.

Per serving: calories: 127, protein: 6 g, fat: 4 g, carbohydrate: 14 g, fiber: 5 g, sodium: 4 mg

Tempeh "Chicken" Salad

YIELD: *2 servings*

Tempeh makes a great stand-in for chicken in this salad, which is an ideal filling for a hearty and chewy sandwich.

1 package (8 ounces) tempeh, cut in half
⅓ to ½ cup vegan mayonnaise
2 green onions, chopped
2 teaspoons poultry seasoning
Optional: 1 tablespoon dried parsley

Fill a medium saucepan about halfway with water. Bring to a boil over high heat. Turn the heat down slightly to maintain a simmer. Add the tempeh, cover, and cook for 10 minutes. Drain. Let cool for 15 minutes.

Mince the tempeh. Then transfer it to a mixing bowl. Add the vegan mayonnaise, green onions, poultry seasoning, and parsley, if using. Stir until thoroughly combined. Transfer to a storage container and refrigerate for at least 1 hour before serving.

Per serving: calories: 443, protein: 21 g, fat: 34 g, carbohydrate: 12 g, fiber: 7 g, sodium: 173 mg

Chickpea-of-the-Sea

YIELD: *3 servings*

This vegan version of tuna salad is based on chopped chickpeas. About half of the people who sampled it said it tastes just like tuna salad—the rest say it's better! I'd love to see this on the menu at every deli and sandwich shop so that everyone—vegan or not—could enjoy this fabulous spread. Don't have a food processor? No problem. Just partially mash the chickpeas with the back of a fork.

1 can (15.5 ounces) chickpeas, rinsed and drained
¼ cup vegan mayonnaise
2 stalks celery, chopped
1½ teaspoons sweet or dill pickle relish
Salt and ground black pepper

Put the chickpeas in a food processor. Pulse 6 times, or until the chickpeas are coarsely chopped. Transfer to a mixing bowl. Add the mayonnaise, celery, and relish. Stir until thoroughly combined. Season with salt and pepper to taste. Serve immediately, or transfer to a storage container and refrigerate until ready to serve.

Chickpea-of-the-Sea with Nori: Tear 1 sheet of nori into 1-inch pieces. Stir the pieces into the salad until evenly distributed.

Per serving: calories: 232, protein: 8 g, fat: 11 g, carbohydrate: 25 g, fiber: 6 g, sodium: 128 mg

6

Dips, Spreads, and Savory Sauces

CHAPTER 6: *Dips, Spreads, and Savory Sauces*

Spinach Dip

YIELD: *3 cups*

Serve this popular party food in a bowl surrounded by crudités or, for a special presentation, hollow out a round loaf of bread and fill it with the dip.

1 container (12 ounces) vegan sour cream
1 package (1½ ounces) instant onion, vegetable, or dill soup or dip mix
1 package (12 ounces) frozen chopped spinach, thawed and drained well
2 tablespoons chopped green onions

Put all of the ingredients in a medium bowl. Stir until thoroughly combined. Transfer to a storage container and refrigerate for at least 1 hour before serving.

Per 2 tablespoons: calories: 44, protein: 1 g, fat: 3 g, carbohydrate: 3 g, fiber: 1 g, sodium: 69 mg

White Bean Nacho Dip

YIELD: *2 3/4 cups*

A great accompaniment to corn chips, this healthful dip blends mild-flavored white beans with rich cashew butter, cheesy-tasting nutritional yeast, and zesty salsa.

1 can (15 ounces) white beans (such as great northern
beans or navy beans), rinsed and drained
1 cup salsa
½ cup nutritional yeast flakes
2 tablespoons cashew butter
Salt

Combine the beans, salsa, nutritional yeast, and cashew butter in a food processor. Process until completely smooth. Season with salt to taste. Serve immediately, or transfer to a storage container and refrigerate until ready to serve.

Per 2 tablespoons: calories: 45, protein: 3 g, fat: 1 g, carbohydrate: 6 g, fiber: 2 g, sodium: 40 mg

Nacho Dip Quesadilla: Place a large flour tortilla in a large skillet over medium-low heat. Spread half of the tortilla with ½ cup of White Bean Nacho Dip. Cook for 1 minute. Fold the tortilla in half over the dip. Gently press the top with a spatula to seal the sides together. The outside of the tortilla should be golden brown but not crispy. Cook either side longer if needed. Slide the quesadilla onto a plate and serve immediately.

Russian Dressing Dip

YIELD: *about ½ cup*

Ketchup and vegan mayonnaise with just a touch of oregano are all you need to make this easy dip. Serve it with a platter of raw vegetables—it's a great way to get fussy eaters (including kids!) to eat their vegetables. You can also use it as a salad dressing or as the perfect condiment for a vegan reuben sandwich.

½ cup vegan mayonnaise
1½ tablespoons ketchup
½ teaspoon dried oregano
½ teaspoon sweet pickle relish

Put all of the ingredients in a small bowl. Stir until thoroughly combined. Serve immediately, or transfer to a storage container and refrigerate until ready to serve.

Per 2 tablespoons: calories: 140, protein: 0 g, fat: 13 g, carbohydrate: 6 g, fiber: 0 g, sodium: 154 mg

Russian Romaine Salad: Top romaine lettuce with Russian Dressing Dip and a sprinkling of nutritional yeast flakes.

Baked Artichoke Dip

YIELD: *3 cups*

This is an outstanding vegan version of the hot and bubbly perennial favorite. Toasted bread rounds, pita chips, or crackers are the perfect accompaniment.

1 package (10 ounces) frozen spinach, thawed and drained well
1 package (9 ounces) frozen artichoke hearts, thawed and drained well
1 cup vegan mayonnaise
2 cloves garlic, minced or pressed
Salt and ground black pepper

Preheat the oven to 350 degrees F. Mist an 8-inch square baking pan with nonstick cooking spray.

Put the spinach, artichoke hearts, mayonnaise, and garlic in a food processor. Pulse several times, until well combined but still chunky. Season with salt and pepper to taste.

Transfer the mixture to the prepared pan. Bake for about 30 minutes, or until bubbly and golden brown. Cool for 5 to 10 minutes before serving.

Per 2 tablespoons: calories: 54, protein: 1 g, fat: 5 g, carbohydrate: 2 g, fiber: 1 g, sodium: 64 mg

Lentil-Walnut Pâté

YIELD: *3 cups*

Luscious and tasty, this pâté is great served with crackers, spread on a sandwich, stuffed into trimmed celery stalks, or mounded on a bed of lettuce.

1 cup dried brown lentils
2 teaspoons extra-virgin olive oil
1 onion, chopped
1 cup chopped walnuts
⅓ cup vegan mayonnaise
Salt

Put the lentils in a heavy saucepan and add enough water to cover by 1 inch. Bring to a boil over high heat. Turn the heat down to low, cover, and cook, stirring occasionally, for about 20 minutes, or until tender. If the lentils start to get dry, add water as needed so they remain soft and moist.

Heat the oil in a small skillet over medium-high heat. Add the onion and cook and stir for about 10 minutes, or until very soft.

Transfer the cooked onion to a food processor. Add the walnuts and lentils. Pulse 5 to 10 times for a chunky spread or process for 30 seconds for a smooth spread, stopping at least once to scrape down the sides of the work bowl.

Transfer to a medium bowl. Stir in the vegan mayonnaise. Season with salt to taste. Transfer to a storage container and refrigerate for at least 2 hours before serving.

Per 2 tablespoons: calories: 75, protein: 3 g, fat: 5 g, carbohydrate: 4 g, fiber: 2 g, sodium: 11 mg

New York–Style Deli Sandwich: Build a thick and hefty sandwich on pumpernickel bread with Lentil Walnut Pâté, vegan coleslaw, and sliced red onion.

Hazelnut-Yam Pâté

YIELD: *3 cups*

In addition to spreading this delicately flavored pâté on crackers and bread, try it as a dip for chips or pretzels. This recipe provides an excellent use for a leftover yam or sweet potato.

½ cup water
⅓ cup hazelnuts
1 cup cooked and mashed yam or sweet potato
¾ cup cooked or canned chickpeas, rinsed and drained
2 teaspoons light miso
Salt and ground black pepper

Combine the water and hazelnuts in a food processor. Process until completely smooth, stopping at least once to scrape down the sides of the blender jar. Add the yam, chickpeas, and miso. Process until creamy. Season with salt and pepper to taste. Serve immediately, or transfer to a storage container and refrigerate until ready to serve.

Per 2 tablespoons: calories: 28, protein: 1 g, fat: 2 g, carbohydrate: 3 g, fiber: 1 g, sodium: 25 mg

Tip: Leftover yams are perfect for this recipe. However, if you have to cook yams specifically for this recipe, you can bake or steam them:
• To bake, pierce each yam twice with a fork or knife, place on aluminum foil, and bake at 375 degrees F for about 45 minutes, or until tender.
• To steam, cut the yams into quarters and place them in a steamer basket over gently boiling water for about 15 minutes, or until tender.

Open-Face Rice Cake: Spread the pâté on rice cakes and top with sliced tomatoes, chopped fresh herbs, and a pinch of salt.

Sundried Tomato Spread

YIELD: *2 cups*

Enjoy the flavors of Tuscany in this tantalizing spread. It's great on crackers or toasted bread rounds. For a delicious twist, toss it with pasta or cooked grains, and serve a side of sautéed or roasted zucchini and a dark green leafy vegetable.

1 jar (6 to 8 ounces) sundried tomatoes packed in oil
1 package (12.3 ounces) firm or extra-firm silken tofu
2 tablespoons freshly squeezed lemon juice
¼ teaspoon salt
⅛ teaspoon ground black pepper
¼ cup fresh basil, tightly packed
1 to 4 tablespoons water, as needed

Drain the sundried tomatoes, reserving the oil. Combine the tofu, lemon juice, salt, pepper, and 2 tablespoons of the tomato oil in a food processor. Process until completely smooth, stopping at least once to scrape down the sides of the work bowl. Add the tomatoes and basil. Pulse 3 to 5 times, until combined but somewhat chunky, adding water as needed to achieve the desired consistency. Serve immediately, or transfer to storage container and refrigerate until ready to serve.

Per 2 tablespoons: calories: 40, protein: 2 g, fat: 2 g, carbohydrate: 3 g, fiber: 1 g, sodium: 80 mg

Black Olive Tapenade

YIELD: *1¼ cups*

Olive lovers will adore this spread, with its rich color and sophisticated flavor. Enjoy it with french bread, roasted garlic, and a glass of red wine.

1 cup pitted kalamata olives
¼ cup capers, rinsed and drained
3 cloves garlic, minced or pressed
¼ cup extra-virgin olive oil
Pinch ground black pepper

Combine the olives, capers, and garlic in a food processor. Process until finely chopped, about 10 seconds. Add the oil and pepper. Process until smooth. Taste and add a bit more pepper, if you like. Serve immediately, or transfer to a storage container and refrigerate until ready to serve.

Per 2 tablespoons: calories: 75, protein: 0 g, fat: 8 g, carbohydrate: 1 g, fiber: 0.5 g, sodium: 204 mg

Roasted Red Bell Pepper Spread

YIELD: *⅔ cup*

With its gorgeous hue and correspondingly vibrant flavor, this spread is sure to impress your party guests. Serve it with bread rounds or crackers or toss it with your favorite pasta for an appetizer or light main dish.

2 red bell peppers
2 tablespoons extra-virgin olive oil
2 to 4 cloves garlic
Red wine vinegar
Salt and ground black pepper

Position an oven rack 3-5 inches below the broiler and preheat the broiler. (The rack should be just low enough from the broiler to accommodate the height of the peppers.)

Arrange the bell peppers on a baking sheet and broil, carefully turning the peppers every few minutes until completely blackened on all sides. Transfer the peppers to a paper bag, close the bag securely, and let sit at room temperature for 30 minutes.

Remove the peppers from the bag. Remove the stems, cut the peppers in half, and remove the seeds. Using your fingers, peel the skins off the peppers (they should come off easily). Coarsely chop the peppers.

Combine the peppers, oil, and garlic in a food processor. Process or pulse until the mixture reaches the desired consistency (it can be smooth or chunky). Season with vinegar, salt, and pepper to taste, being careful not to overdo the pepper. Serve immediately, or transfer to a storage container and refrigerate until ready to serve.

Per 2 tablespoons: calories: 60, protein: 0.5 g, fat: 6 g, carbohydrate: 2 g, fiber: 1 g, sodium: 2 mg

Vineyard Peppers

YIELD: *2 cups*

Scoop up these peppers with crusty french bread or serve them with crackers or crostini. They are also delicious tossed with freshly cooked penne.

3 bell peppers, preferably of various colors
1 banana pepper
3 tablespoons extra-virgin olive oil
¼ teaspoon balsamic vinegar
1 tablespoon minced garlic
Salt and ground black pepper

Position an oven rack 3-5 inches below the broiler and preheat the broiler. (The rack should be just low enough from the broiler to accommodate the height of the peppers.)

Arrange the bell peppers and banana pepper on a baking sheet and broil, carefully turning the peppers every few minutes until completely blackened on all sides. Transfer the peppers to a paper bag, close the bag securely, and let sit at room temperature for 30 minutes.

Remove the peppers from the bag. Remove the stems, cut the peppers in half, and remove the seeds. Using your fingers, peel the skins off the peppers (they should come off easily). Cut the peppers into strips about 3 inches long and ½ inch wide.

Put the pepper strips in a medium bowl. Add the oil, vinegar, and garlic. Stir gently until the peppers are thoroughly coated. Season with salt and pepper to taste. Serve immediately, or transfer to a storage container and refrigerate until ready to serve.

Per 2 tablespoons: calories: 30, protein: 0.5 g, fat: 3 g, carbohydrate: 1 g, fiber: 1 g, sodium: 2 mg

Creamy Horseradish Dipping Sauce

YIELD: *about ½ cup*

This recipe, strong in flavor yet rich and luscious on the tongue, was developed to accompany Crispy Artichoke Hearts (page 106). It's also a great topping for brown rice and steamed cruciferous vegetables, such as broccoli, cabbage, and cauliflower.

¼ cup vegan sour cream
¼ cup vegan prepared horseradish
1 tablespoon vegan mayonnaise
¾ teaspoon Dijon mustard
⅛ teaspoon salt

Put all of the ingredients in a small bowl. Stir or whisk until thoroughly combined. Serve immediately, or transfer to a storage container and refrigerate until ready to serve.

Per 2 tablespoons: calories: 55, protein: 1 g, fat: 5 g, carbohydrate: 3 g, fiber: 5 g, sodium: 165 mg

Agave-Mustard Dipping Sauce

YIELD: *about 3/4 cup*

This sweet and zippy mustard sauce makes an excellent dip for Crispy Artichoke Hearts (page 106). Also try it with zucchini sticks, baked sweet potato fries, or any other vegetables you like to dip.

½ cup vegan mayonnaise
2 tablespoons yellow mustard
1 to 1½ tablespoons agave nectar

Put all of the ingredients in a small bowl. Stir or whisk until thoroughly combined. Serve immediately, or transfer to a storage container and refrigerate until ready to serve.

Per 2 tablespoons: calories: 106, protein: 0 g, fat: 9 g, carbohydrate: 7 g, fiber: 0 g, sodium: 126 mg

Creamy Dijon Dipping Sauce

YIELD: *about ½ cup*

Try this all-purpose sauce on broiled tempeh, baked tofu, or beans and brown rice, or use it as a dip for Crispy Artichoke Hearts (page 106).

½ cup vegan mayonnaise
1 tablespoon Dijon mustard
1 teaspoon sweet or dill pickle relish

Put all of the ingredients in a small bowl. Stir or whisk until thoroughly combined. Serve immediately, or transfer to a storage container and refrigerate until ready to serve.

Per 2 tablespoons: calories: 148, protein: 0 g, fat: 14 g, carbohydrate: 6 g, fiber: 0 g, sodium: 278 mg

Peanut Sauce and Dip

YIELD: *about 1¼ cups*

Rich and slightly sweet, this highly versatile sauce lends an Asian flair to pasta, cooked grains, roasted or steamed vegetables, baked tofu, or grilled or broiled tempeh or seitan. It's especially tasty tossed with brown rice and steamed broccoli or kale, or try it with penne, peas, and green onions. It couldn't be easier to make, and it doesn't even require heating.

½ cup smooth unsalted peanut butter
½ cup water
3 tablespoons agave nectar
1 clove garlic, minced or pressed
1 teaspoon tamari

Put all of the ingredients in a medium bowl. Stir or whisk until thoroughly combined. Serve immediately, or transfer to a storage container and refrigerate until ready to serve.

Per 2 tablespoons: calories: 95, protein: 4 g, fat: 6 g, carbohydrate: 8 g, fiber: 1 g, sodium: 35 mg

Tip: The sauce will thicken after it has been refrigerated. To thin, stir in a small amount of water, 2 teaspoons at a time, until the desired consistency is achieved. If desired, the sauce can be heated in a small saucepan over very low heat; stir constantly to prevent burning.

Cashew "Cheese" Sauce

YIELD: *2 cups*

This all-purpose, five-minute cheese sauce imparts the sensory experience of Alfredo sauce without the saturated fat and cholesterol found in traditional cream-based recipes. Plus, it's extremely versatile. Try it over pasta with vegetables, beans, or both; over short-grain brown rice with steamed broccoli; on roasted potatoes with white beans and steamed kale; or tossed with elbow macaroni for delicious old-fashioned mac and "cheese."

¾ cup raw cashews
¾ cup water
⅓ cup nutritional yeast flakes
2 tablespoons light miso
¼ teaspoon salt

Combine the cashews and water in a blender. Process until completely smooth, with no cashew pieces remaining, stopping at least once to scrape down the sides of the blender jar. Add the nutritional yeast, miso, and salt. Process until smooth. Serve immediately, or transfer to a storage container and refrigerate until ready to serve.

Per 2 tablespoons: calories: 49, protein: 3 g, fat: 3 g, carbohydrate: 3 g, fiber: 1 g, sodium: 86 mg

Tip: For quick macaroni and "cheese," cook elbow macaroni in boiling water until tender. Drain and transfer to a saucepan. Stir in Cashew "Cheese" Sauce to taste. Heat gently, stirring occasionally, until warmed through. Cashew "Cheese" Sauce can be added to grain, vegetable, or bean mixtures while they are still in the saucepan or skillet. Simply stir in the sauce and heat gently.

Butternut Sauce

YIELD: *2 cups*

This rich, creamy sauce transforms butternut squash into a golden, cheesy topping for elbow macaroni or steamed vegetables.

1 small butternut squash, peeled, seeded, and cut into ¾-inch chunks (see tip)
¼ cup nutritional yeast flakes
2 tablespoons tahini
2 teaspoons light miso
½ teaspoon salt

Put the butternut squash in a steamer basket over simmering water. Steam for about 12 minutes, or until tender.

Put 2 cups of the steamed squash in a food processor. (Enjoy the remaining squash as is, or refrigerate it for later use.) Add the nutritional yeast, tahini, miso, and salt. Process until completely smooth, stopping at least once to scrape down the sides of the work bowl. Serve immediately, or transfer to a storage container and refrigerate until ready to serve.

Per ¼ cup: calories: 93, protein: 4 g, fat: 4 g, carbohydrate: 11 g, fiber: 2 g, sodium: 365 mg

Tip: To prepare the squash, start by slicing off and discarding the two ends. Using a small spoon, scrape the seeds out of the bulbous end. Peel away the skin using a sturdy vegetable peeler. Cut the flesh into chunks.

Baked Potato Topped with Butternut Broccoli: Toss steamed broccoli with Butternut Sauce. Use as a topping for hot, fluffy baked potatoes.

Penne with Greens and Butternut Sauce: Toss freshly cooked penne with steamed asparagus, spinach, and Butternut Sauce.

Bolognese Sauce

YIELD: *5½ cups*

Although this sauce is high in protein, thanks to the textured vegetable protein, it's extremely low in fat, so you can be generous when you ladle it over pasta or add it to your favorite lasagne recipe.

1 tablespoon extra-virgin olive oil
1 onion, finely chopped
8 ounces mushrooms, thinly sliced (about 3 cups)
1 jar (16 ounces) vegan spaghetti sauce
1½ cups water
1 cup textured vegetable protein
Salt and ground black pepper

Heat the oil in a heavy saucepan over medium-high heat. Add the onion and cook and stir for about 7 minutes, or until softened. Add the mushrooms and cook and stir for about 5 minutes, or until softened. Add the spaghetti sauce and water and stir well. Bring to a simmer. Turn the heat down to low, cover, and cook for 10 minutes, stirring occasionally.

Remove from the heat. Stir in the textured vegetable protein. Cover and let sit for 15 minutes. Season with salt and pepper to taste. If necessary, warm over low heat before serving.

Per ½ cup: calories: 79, protein: 5 g, fat: 3 g, carbohydrate: 6 g, fiber: 2 g, sodium: 172 mg

Italian Sausage and Pepper Sauce

YIELD: *4 servings*

Vegan sausage is the perfect enhancement for this Italian-inspired dish, complementing the onions, peppers, and spaghetti sauce. Traditionally served over pasta, this chunky meal-in-a-sauce is also satisfying over rice and other grains.

1 tablespoon extra-virgin olive oil
1 package (16 ounces) vegan sausages, sliced ½ inch thick (or thicker, if desired)
1 large onion, cut in half and sliced into half-moons
2 red or green bell peppers, cut into 2-inch squares
1 jar (16 ounces) vegan spaghetti sauce
Optional: nutritional yeast flakes

Heat the oil in a medium nonstick skillet or heavy saucepan over medium-high heat. Add the vegan sausages and cook and stir for about 7 minutes, or until browned. Add the onion and cook and stir for 7 minutes. Add the bell peppers and cook and stir for about 5 minutes, or until softened. Add the spaghetti sauce. Stir gently and bring to a simmer. Turn the heat down to low, cover, and cook for 15 minutes.

Serve garnished with a sprinkling of nutritional yeast, if desired.

Per serving: calories: 323, protein: 25 g, fat: 14 g, carbohydrate: 19 g, fiber: 8 g, sodium: 1,225 mg

Sausage and Pepper Grinders: Serve the sauce in toasted grinder rolls. (Grinders are also known as submarine sandwiches or hoagies.)

7

Main Dishes

CHAPTER 7: *Main Dishes*

Mediterranean Penne

YIELD: *4 servings*

Capers are a distinctive ingredient often used in Mediterranean cooking. In this recipe, they're tossed with penne and a blend of tahini and vegan mayonnaise for a quick dish with a bold, exquisite flavor.

1 pound penne
½ cup tahini
⅓ cup vegan mayonnaise
2 tablespoons capers, rinsed and drained

Cook the penne in boiling water until tender.

Meanwhile, put the tahini and vegan mayonnaise in a large bowl. Stir until thoroughly combined, with no lumps. (Do not overstir, as it will cause oil separation).

Drain the penne. While it's still hot and steamy, add it to the tahini mixture along with the capers. Toss gently until the penne is thoroughly coated. Serve immediately, otherwise the penne will soak up too much of the moisture in the sauce.

Per serving: calories: 677, protein: 20 g, fat: 25 g, carbohydrate: 93 g, fiber: 6 g, sodium: 219 mg

Penne with Zucchini: Chop 2 zucchini and cook them in a little extra-virgin olive oil over medium-high heat, just until tender. Add them to the tahini mixture along with the cooked penne.

Linguine with Sea Greens

YIELD: *4 servings*

This combination of spaghetti sauce and sea vegetables ladled over pasta is an absolute must for anyone whose senses are enlivened by the sea. Use your favorite vegan spaghetti sauce or experiment with spicy versions to heighten the flavor. Linguine goes especially well with this dish, but any pasta will work just fine.

1 jar (16 ounces) vegan spaghetti sauce
½ cup water
1 package (about 1 ounce) mixed dried sea vegetables (see tip)
1 pound linguine

Pour the spaghetti sauce into a medium saucepan. Pour the water into the empty spaghetti sauce jar, screw the cover on tightly, and shake well. Pour into the spaghetti sauce and stir well. Bring to a simmer over medium-high heat. Remove from the heat, stir in the sea vegetables, cover, and let sit for 15 minutes. If necessary, warm over low heat before serving.

Meanwhile, cook the linguine in boiling water until tender. Drain. Transfer the linguine to a large bowl. Add the sauce, toss well, and serve immediately.

Per serving: calories: 306, protein: 18 g, fat: 4 g, carbohydrate: 95 g, fiber: 5 g, sodium: 513 mg

Tip: Packages of mixed dried sea vegetables (sometimes called ocean greens) are sold in most natural food stores. The blend usually contains about six different varieties of sea vegetables, all of which increase substantially in size as they rehydrate in the spaghetti sauce. You can also purchase a wide variety of sea vegetables at natural food stores or online and make your own mix.

Roasted Eggplant and Pesto Roulade

YIELD: *6 servings*

This elegant and flavorful dish made of roasted eggplant slices rolled up around a pesto filling and baked in spaghetti sauce is a sight to behold. A crisp green salad and a green vegetable on the side are the perfect accompaniments.

2 large eggplants, ends trimmed
1 package (1 pound) firm or extra-firm regular tofu, rinsed and drained
2 cups store-bought vegan pesto
2 jars (26 ounces each) vegan spaghetti sauce

Position an oven rack a few inches under the broiler and preheat the broiler. Mist a baking sheet with nonstick cooking spray.

Working with one at a time, stand the eggplants up vertically with the larger side on the bottom and slice them from top to bottom, making somewhat thin slices about ¼ inch thick. This should yield about 20 slices in all.

Place the slices on the prepared pan and mist them with nonstick cooking spray (preferably olive oil spray). Broil for 2 to 3 minutes, or until golden brown. Turn the slices over and broil for 2 to 3 minutes longer, or until golden brown. Watch carefully to avoid overbrowning or crisping the eggplant. Remove the eggplant from the oven and let it cool.

Lower the oven temperature to 350 degrees F. Lightly mist a 9 x 11-inch baking pan with nonstick cooking spray.

Put the tofu in a medium bowl and mash it well with a potato masher or the back of a fork. Add the pesto and stir until thoroughly combined.

Spread the pesto mixture over each roasted eggplant slice about ¼ inch thick, leaving the top inch of the narrow end uncovered. Roll up each slice, starting with the large end. (The top of the narrow end will form a nice seal, since it isn't covered with the tofu mixture.) If any of the eggplant slices are too short to roll, simply top them with the filling and fold them over into "clamshells." Place each roll seam-side down in the prepared pan. Nestle them together and spoon the spaghetti sauce over the top, pouring any extra sauce around and between the rolls. Bake for about 35 minutes, or until bubbly.

Per serving: calories: 452, protein: 11 g, fat: 36 g, carbohydrate: 19 g, fiber: 6 g, sodium: 1,019 mg

Ravioli with Broccoli in Coconut Sauce

YIELD: *2 servings*

If you've yet to try any of the vegan ravioli available in the freezer section of most natural food stores, you're in for a treat. This recipe offers an unusual twist, combining this Italian favorite with coconut milk and peanuts for Thai-inspired flavor. Butternut squash ravioli complements these ingredients perfectly, but feel free to experiment with other varieties if you like, such as roasted red pepper or wild mushroom.

1 can (14 ounces) coconut milk

2 cups broccoli florets, or 1 package (10 ounces) frozen chopped broccoli, thawed and drained well

1 package (13 to 15 ounces) frozen butternut squash ravioli

2 tablespoons finely chopped peanuts

Put the coconut milk in a medium saucepan over medium-high heat and bring to a simmer. Gently stir in the broccoli and ravioli. Cover and cook for 8 minutes, or until a fork inserted through the center of a ravioli comes out hot. Transfer to a serving bowl or individual pasta bowls. Top with the peanuts.

Per serving: calories: 693, protein: 15 g, fat: 52 g, carbohydrate: 46 g, fiber: 9 g, sodium: 503 mg

Ravioli with Spinach in Coconut Sauce: Omit the broccoli and gently fold in 4 cups of baby spinach during the last 2 minutes of cooking.

One-Pot Lentil-Vegetable Supper

YIELD: *4 to 6 servings*

Lentils and vegetables make for a humble yet wholesome dish. This easy recipe is mildly seasoned, but you can jazz it up as you like with herbs, hot sauce, or tamari. Serve it in bowls as a stew or over cooked grains or pasta. Chilled, it makes a hearty salad.

1 tablespoon extra-virgin olive oil
4 cups bite-size mixed fresh vegetables (see tip)
1 carton (32 ounces) vegetable broth
1 can (28 ounces) chopped tomatoes
2½ cups dried brown lentils
Salt and ground black pepper

Heat the oil in a heavy soup pot over medium-high heat. Add the vegetables and cook and stir for about 7 minutes, or until slightly browned. Stir in the broth, tomatoes, and lentils. Bring to a boil. Turn the heat down to low, cover, and simmer for about 50 minutes, or until the lentils are tender. Season with salt and pepper to taste before serving.

Per serving: calories: 374, protein: 25 g, fat: 4 g, carbohydrate: 43 g, fiber: 25 g, sodium: 312 mg

Tip: Recommended vegetables include broccoli, carrots, cauliflower, celery, collard greens, green beans, kale, onions, sweet potatoes, and zucchini. Frozen vegetables don't work well in this recipe because they tend to add a significant amount of water to the dish, causing it to be somewhat runny.

Stuffed Bell Peppers

YIELD: *4 servings*

This flavorful and colorful dish is a perfect example of how just a few common ingredients can be combined to make a fun and interesting meal. Parboiling the peppers and cooking the rice add a bit of preparation time, but the dish is still very easy to make and well worth the extra effort.

1 cup water
½ cup brown rice
4 red bell peppers
1 can (14.7 ounces) vegan chili
1½ to 2 cups salsa
Optional: nutritional yeast flakes

Combine the water and rice in a small saucepan over medium-high heat and bring to a boil. Turn the heat down to low, cover, and cook for about 45 minutes, or until the water is absorbed.

Meanwhile, bring a large pot of water to a boil. Set a cooling rack on top of a kitchen towel.

Slice the tops off the peppers and discard the stems (save the rest of the tops for salad or another use). Carefully remove the seeds and membranes, keeping the peppers intact. Lower the peppers into the boiling water and cook for 1 minute. Transfer the peppers to the cooling rack, placing them upside down to drain.

Preheat the oven to 350 degrees F.

Combine the chili and rice in a medium bowl and mix well. Spread ½ cup of the salsa over the bottom of an 8-inch square baking pan. Place the peppers in the pan upright and fill them with the chili mixture. Spoon the remaining salsa over the peppers. Sprinkle with nutritional yeast, if using.

Cover with foil and bake for about 30 minutes, or until bubbly. Cool for 5 minutes before serving.

Per serving: calories: 213, protein: 9 g, fat: 1 g, carbohydrate: 34 g, fiber: 11 g, sodium: 457 mg

New-Fashioned Greens and Black-Eyed Peas

YIELD: *3 servings*

The traditional method of preparing collard greens and black-eyed peas involves hours of boiling, not to mention the unfortunate addition of animal fat. Here, this quintessential Southern dish has been updated to require minimal cooking time. Vegan worcestershire sauce adds just the right note of tangy flavor.

1 tablespoon extra-virgin olive oil
2 to 4 cloves garlic, minced or pressed
1 large bunch collard greens, trimmed and coarsely chopped (about 6 cups)
2 cans (15 ounces each) black-eyed peas, rinsed and drained
¼ cup vegan worcestershire sauce
Salt and ground black pepper

Heat the oil in a large, heavy pot over medium-high heat. Add the garlic and cook and stir for 30 seconds. Add the collard greens and cook and stir for about 5 minutes, or until bright green and slightly tender. Add the black-eyed peas and worcestershire sauce and mix well. Bring to a boil. Turn the heat down to low, cover, and cook, stirring occasionally, for about 20 minutes, or until the greens are tender to your liking. Season generously with salt and pepper before serving.

Per serving: calories: 179, protein: 8 g, fat: 1 g, carbohydrate: 26 g, fiber: 10 g, sodium: 956 mg

Indian Chickpeas, Cauliflower, and Potatoes

YIELD: *3 servings*

You don't need a host of special spices to create tantalizing Indian food; just stock your pantry with a jar or two of Indian-inspired simmer sauce. Check the international aisle of your supermarket or natural food store for vegan options, reading labels carefully to make sure they don't contain any animal products, such as cream or ghee (clarified butter). This dish is particularly good served over brown basmati rice with a fruit chutney on the side.

1 tablespoon extra-virgin olive oil
1 head cauliflower, cut into bite-size florets (about 3 cups)
1 large potato, peeled and cut into ½-inch chunks
1 can (15.5 ounces) chickpeas, rinsed and drained
1 jar (14 to 18 ounces) vegan Indian simmer sauce
½ cup water

Heat the oil in a large, heavy saucepan over medium-high heat. Add the cauliflower and potato. Cook and stir for about 7 minutes, or until the cauliflower begins to soften. Stir in the chickpeas and simmer sauce. Bring to a boil. Turn the heat down to low, cover, and cook for 40 minutes, stirring occasionally and adding the water about halfway through the cooking time. Remove from the heat. Let sit for 10 minutes before serving.

Per serving: calories: 273, protein: 11 g, fat: 8 g, carbohydrate: 38 g, fiber: 10 g, sodium: 50 mg

South-of-the-Border Quesadilla

YIELD: *1 serving*

Roasted red pepper hummus makes a surprisingly good stand-in for melted cheese in this Mexican fast-food specialty. This recipe can easily be doubled, tripled, or quadrupled, depending on the number of people you need to serve (or how hungry you are).

1 large flour tortilla
⅓ cup roasted red pepper hummus
⅓ cup salsa (see tip)
¼ cup guacamole

Heat a large, dry skillet over medium heat. Lay the tortilla in the pan and spread half of the tortilla with the hummus and the other half with the salsa. Cook for about 1½ minutes. Fold the hummus half over the salsa half and gently press down on the top of the quesadilla with a spatula to seal the sides together. The outside of the tortilla should be golden brown but not crispy. Cook either side longer if needed. Slide the quesadilla onto a plate and dollop the top with the guacamole.

Per serving: calories: 400, protein: 7 g, fat: 19 g, carbohydrate: 45 g, fiber: 8 g, sodium: 943 mg

Tip: When measuring out the salsa, try to keep as much of the salsa liquid out of the measuring cup as possible to avoid a soggy or dripping quesadilla.

Black Bean Roll-Ups

YIELD: *6 servings*

Who would guess that such an easy recipe could yield tasty south-of-the-border fare? Sautéed vegetables and black beans are rolled into soft tortillas and baked in salsa until piping hot, making for a satisfying entrée akin to enchiladas. For a festive presentation, garnish them with guacamole, vegan sour cream, and chopped green onions.

2 jars (16 ounces each) salsa
1 tablespoon extra-virgin olive oil
3 cups bite-size mixed vegetables (such as broccoli, kale, onion,
    red bell pepper, or zucchini)
2 cans (15 ounces each) black beans, rinsed and drained
6 to 8 large flour tortillas

Preheat the oven to 350 degrees F. Spread ½ cup of the salsa over the bottom of an 8 x 11-inch baking pan.

Heat the oil in a large skillet over medium-high heat. Add the vegetables and cook and stir for about 7 minutes, or until tender. Stir in the beans and remove from the heat.

Place a tortilla on a work surface. Spoon about ⅔ cup of the vegetable mixture in a line across the middle of the tortilla. Roll the tortilla around the filling and place it seam-side down in the baking pan. Repeat with the remaining tortillas. Cover the roll-ups with the remaining salsa, spreading it evenly over the tortillas with the back of a spoon. Spoon any remaining filling onto and around the roll-ups.

Cover with foil and bake for about 35 minutes, or until bubbly.

Per serving: calories: 301, protein: 12 g, fat: 4 g, carbohydrate: 51 g, fiber: 13 g, sodium: 635 mg

Pierogies Italiano

YIELD: *3 servings*

The instructions on most store-bought pierogies recommend sautéing or boiling for optimal results. However, simmering pierogies in spaghetti sauce yields equally fabulous texture—and an unusual yet spectacular Polish-Italian fusion. The broccoli and fresh basil provide a bright, fresh flavor that complements the dish perfectly.

1 jar (26 ounces) vegan spaghetti sauce
3 cups fresh or frozen broccoli florets
1 package (14 ounces) vegan pierogies (preferably potato-spinach; see tip)
3 tablespoons chopped fresh basil

Pour the spaghetti sauce into a large pot. Bring to a simmer over medium-high heat. Stir in the broccoli. Turn the heat down to low, cover, and cook for 10 minutes if using fresh broccoli or 5 minutes if using frozen broccoli.

Carefully add the pierogies one at a time, using a wooden spoon to nudge them under the sauce as much as possible. Cover and cook for 20 minutes, carefully stirring every 5 to 10 minutes to ensure that the pierogies cook on all sides and don't stick to the bottom of the pot.

Stir in the basil during the last 5 minutes of cooking. Let cool for 5 minutes before serving.

Per serving: calories: 347, protein: 11 g, fat: 8 g, carbohydrate: 57 g, fiber: 5 g, sodium: 1,468 mg

Tip: Most large supermarkets carry a selection of fresh pierogies in the same refrigerated section as pizza dough, pizza, and premade sandwiches. Look for vegan varieties, such as potato, potato-onion, and potato-spinach.

Tomato and Yam Pizza

YIELD: *4 servings*

This surprisingly tasty pizza is topped with an unusual combination: yams, tomato, and hummus. And with french bread serving as the crust, it's a snap to make.

1 (14-inch) baguette
2 large yams, cooked (see tip), peeled or unpeeled, and thinly sliced
1 tomato, thinly sliced
1 cup hummus, any flavor

Preheat the oven to 350 degrees F. Slice the baguette in half lengthwise and then across to make 4 pieces. Place the pieces crust-side down in an 8-inch square baking pan. The pieces should fit snugly to keep them from rolling.

Layer the yam slices on the bread. Top with the tomato. Spread the hummus over the tomato. Bake for about 15 minutes, or until the edges of the bread are toasted.

Per serving: calories: 416, protein: 14 g, fat: 7 g, carbohydrate: 65 g, fiber: 9 g, sodium: 710 mg

Tip: Leftover yams are perfect for this recipe. However, if you have to cook them specifically for the pizza, you have several options—baking, roasting, or steaming:

- To bake, preheat the oven to 375 degrees F. Pierce each yam twice with a fork or knife, place on aluminum foil, and bake for about 45 minutes, or until tender. Cool before slicing.

- To roast, preheat the oven to 375 degrees F. Slice the yams and place them on a lightly oiled baking sheet. Mist the yams with nonstick cooking spray and roast for about 20 minutes, or until browned.

- To steam, thinly slice the yams. Place them in a steamer basket over gently boiling water for about 12 minutes, or until tender.

Pizza Verde

YIELD: *2 servings*

Most natural food stores and natural food sections of large supermarkets carry a selection of high-quality frozen vegan pizzas. This recipe showcases just one of many ways to transform this fast-food favorite into a fabulous and healthful meal by heaping it with a generous amount of antioxidant-rich vegetables.

3 cups bite-size mixed fresh or frozen vegetables (such as broccoli, red bell pepper, and zucchini)
4 teaspoons extra-virgin olive oil
1 small bunch kale, chopped (about 3 cups)
1 vegan frozen pizza

Preheat the oven to 375 degrees F. Mist a baking sheet with nonstick cooking spray.

Put the mixed vegetables in a large bowl. Drizzle with 2 teaspoons of the oil. Stir gently to coat. Spread the vegetables in a single layer on the prepared baking sheet. Roast for about 25 minutes, or until tender and browned.

Meanwhile, heat the remaining 2 teaspoons of oil in a skillet over medium-high heat. Add the kale and cook and stir for 3 to 5 minutes, or until slightly tender and bright green.

Prepare the pizza according to the package directions. As soon as you remove it from the oven, cover it with the roasted vegetables and the kale. Pack the vegetables down slightly using the back of a spoon. Slice into quarters and serve immediately.

Per serving: calories: 365, protein: 14 g, fat: 12 g, carbohydrate: 49 g, fiber: 13 g, sodium: 288 mg

Tip: You can bake the pizza in the oven together with the vegetables. If the pizza needs to be baked at a higher temperature, just roast the vegetables for a shorter time and stir them occasionally as needed. Or, to save more time, cook the mixed vegetables together with the kale instead of roasting them.

Classic-Style Pierogies

YIELD: *3 servings*

In this recipe, pierogies are prepared in the traditional Polish fashion: with sautéed onions and mushrooms and a dollop of sour cream (vegan, of course). This is hearty comfort food that will warm you up on a cold evening.

1 tablespoon extra-virgin olive oil

1 onion, thinly sliced

8 ounces mushrooms (any variety or a combination), sliced (about 3 cups)

1 package (14 ounces) vegan pierogies (see tip, page 84)

⅓ cup vegan sour cream

Heat the oil in a large, nonstick skillet or heavy skillet over medium-high heat. Add the onion and cook and stir for about 7 minutes, or until softened and browned. Add the mushrooms and cook and stir for about 5 minutes, or until tender.

Add the pierogies and nestle them under the vegetables so they're directly on the surface of the skillet. Cook for about 5 minutes, until browned. Turn the pierogies over and cook for about 5 minutes longer, until browned on the other side. Top each serving with a dollop of vegan sour cream. Serve immediately.

Per serving: calories: 314, protein: 9 g, fat: 12 g, carbohydrate: 45 g, fiber: 3 g, sodium: 472 mg

Barbecue Tempeh

YIELD: *2 servings*

Equally well suited to a backyard picnic in summer or a dinner by the fire in winter, this is a great year-round dish. Onions and bell peppers provide tender contrast to succulent tempeh, with a backdrop of zesty barbecue sauce to meld everything together. Serve with roasted potatoes and a crisp green salad for a delightfully scrumptious meal. This dish is also excellent over brown rice or as a topping for a baked potato—or just on its own.

1 package (8 ounces) tempeh, cut in half
1½ tablespoons extra-virgin olive oil
1 large onion, chopped
1 red or green bell pepper, chopped
1 to 2 cups barbecue sauce

Fill a medium saucepan about halfway with water. Bring to a boil over high heat. Turn the heat down slightly to maintain a simmer. Add the tempeh, cover, and cook for 10 minutes. Drain. Let cool for 15 minutes.

Heat 1 tablespoon of the oil in a large skillet over medium-high heat. Add the onion and bell pepper. Cook and stir for about 7 minutes, or until softened and lightly browned. Cut the tempeh into 1-inch cubes and add it to the vegetables. Cook and stir for about 7 minutes, or until the tempeh starts to brown, adding up to ½ tablespoon more oil if it starts to stick.

Stir in 1 cup of the barbecue sauce and bring to a simmer. Turn the heat down to low, cover, and cook, stirring occasionally, for 30 minutes, adding more barbecue sauce, ¼ cup at a time, if the mixture starts to stick to the bottom of the pan. Serve immediately.

Per serving: calories: 595, protein: 26 g, fat: 26 g, carbohydrate: 63 g, fiber: 18 g, sodium: 2,055 mg

Seitan with Tomatoes and Sauerkraut

YIELD: *4 to 6 servings*

Tomatoes, sauerkraut, and sour cream form a surprisingly delicious trio, especially in this chunky sauce over seitan. Although this recipe takes just a few minutes to prepare, it's extremely flavorful and satisfying.

1 tablespoon extra-virgin olive oil
2 pounds chicken-style or plain seitan, drained well
    and cut into bite-size chunks (about 3 cups)
2 large tomatoes, coarsely chopped
½ cup drained sauerkraut
2 tablespoons vegan sour cream

Heat the oil in a large, nonstick or heavy skillet over medium-high heat. Add the seitan and cook and stir for about 7 minutes, or until lightly browned. Add the tomatoes and cook and stir for about 2 minutes, or until most of their juices evaporate. Add the sauerkraut and cook and stir for 2 minutes. Remove from the heat. Stir in the vegan sour cream and serve immediately.

Per serving: calories: 729, protein: 138 g, fat: 7 g, carbohydrate: 28 g, fiber: 3 g, sodium: 224 mg

Vegan Sausage with Tomatoes and Sauerkraut: Replace the seitan with 2 pounds of vegan sausages, sliced into ⅓-inch rounds.

Hefty Greens

YIELD: *2 servings*

In this recipe, water chestnuts and vegan ground sausage lend substance and superb flavor to leafy greens, transforming them from a side dish into a hearty and healthful main dish.

6 cups chopped leafy green vegetables (such as bok choy, mustard greens, or spinach)
1 cup water
2 teaspoons extra-virgin olive oil
14 ounces vegan ground sausage (about 2 cups), crumbled or chopped
    into bite-size chunks (see tip)
1 can (8-ounces) sliced water chestnuts, drained
1 tablespoon tamari

Combine the vegetables and water in a large saucepan. Bring to a boil over high heat. Turn the heat down to low and cook for 1 minute, or until the greens turn bright green. Drain well.

Heat the olive oil in a large skillet over medium-high heat. Add the vegan sausage and water chestnuts. Cook and stir for 5 to 7 minutes, or until browned. Add the drained vegetables and tamari. Cook and stir for about 5 minutes, or until the mixture is hot and the greens are tender to your liking. Serve immediately.

Per serving: calories: 550, protein: 57 g, fat: 21 g, carbohydrate: 27 g, fiber: 18 g, sodium: 1,952 mg

Tip: Vegan sausage is available ground or in links; either is fine in this recipe. If using ground sausage, break off chunks using your fingers. If using sausage links, slice or chop them with a knife.

Hefty Greens Sandwich: Top 2 slices of whole-grain bread with vegan mayonnaise and sprinkle lightly with nutritional yeast flakes. Spoon ½ cup of Hefty Greens (warm or cold) on one of the prepared bread slices, cover with the other slice, and enjoy!

Spinach Casserole

YIELD: *4 servings*

Layers of delicate phyllo dough envelope a melange of potatoes, nutritional yeast, and spinach to create this Mediterranean-inspired comfort food.

6 potatoes, scrubbed and cut into large chunks
2 pounds spinach, chopped
6 tablespoons nutritional yeast flakes
½ teaspoon salt
16 sheets phyllo dough (see tip)
¼ cup extra-virgin olive oil, or as needed

Fill a large saucepan halfway with water and bring to a boil over high heat. Add the potatoes and cook for about 10 minutes, or until fork-tender. Drain the potatoes and return them to the saucepan or transfer them to a large bowl.

Mash potatoes with a potato masher or the back of a fork until the desired consistency is achieved (the potatoes can be smooth or lumpy). Stir in the spinach, nutritional yeast, and salt.

Preheat the oven to 375 degrees F. Lightly mist an 8-inch square baking pan with nonstick cooking spray.

Place a sheet of phyllo in the bottom of the prepared baking dish, allowing the excess to drape over the edge, and brush with a light coating of the oil. Repeat this layering process for a total of 8 sheets of phyllo dough.

Spread the potato filling over the phyllo dough and use a fork or the back of a spoon to lightly pack the mixture and smooth the top. Lay a sheet of phyllo dough over the filling, allowing the excess to drape over the edge, and brush with a light coating of oil. Repeat for a total of 8 sheets on top of the filling.

Fold the edges of the phyllo dough over the top layer and brush the very top with a light coating of oil.

Bake for about 30 minutes, or until the top is flaky and golden brown.

Per serving: calories: 651, protein: 26 g, fat: 16 g, carbohydrate: 104 g, fiber: 15 g, sodium: 762 mg

Tip: It's important to work efficiently and carefully with phyllo dough because it dries out quickly and tears easily. Follow these steps for optimal results:

1. Stack the phyllo sheets needed for the recipe on a piece of parchment paper or waxed paper.

2. Drape a damp kitchen cloth over the stack; make sure it isn't too wet, as this can cause the layers to stick together.

3. Uncover the phyllo sheets as you need them, quickly replacing the damp cloth over the stack after you remove each sheet.

4. If a piece tears, you can still use it. Just piece it together as best you can. Make sure to keep one intact sheet for a great-looking top.

5. To reduce the fat content, mist each sheet of phyllo dough with olive oil spray instead of brushing it with olive oil.

Stuffed Onion Casserole

YIELD: *6 servings*

If you like onions, you'll love the assertive flavor of this casserole. Onions are hollowed out to form little bowls, filled with a delicious mix of peas, spinach, and amaranth, then cooked until soft and succulent.

5 cups water
1 cup green split peas
1 cup amaranth
6 large red onions
1 tablespoon extra-virgin olive oil
1 bunch spinach, chopped
½ teaspoon salt
¼ teaspoon ground black pepper

Pour 3 cups of the water into a medium saucepan. Add the split peas and bring to a boil over high heat. Turn the heat down to low, cover, and cook for about 45 minutes, or until the water is almost completely absorbed.

Meanwhile, pour the remaining 2 cups of water into a medium saucepan. Add the amaranth and bring to boil over high heat. Turn the heat down to low, cover, and cook, stirring occasionally, for 20 to 25 minutes, or until the water is absorbed.

Trim off both ends of the onions. Carefully peel the onions, cut them in half around the middle, and hollow out the centers with a spoon, leaving only the outer three layers of each onion. Reserve the onion centers.

Preheat the oven to 350 degrees F. Lightly mist an 8 x 11-inch baking pan with nonstick cooking spray. Place the onions in the pan, open-side up (like little bowls). The onions should fill the pan, which will prevent them from rolling.

Chop the onion centers. Heat the oil in a medium skillet over medium-high heat. Add the chopped onions and cook and stir for 10 to 15 minutes, or until golden brown.

Stir the spinach into the split peas and cook over low heat, stirring occasionally, for about 5 minutes, or until all of the liquid is absorbed. Remove from the heat before the mixture begins to stick to the bottom of the pot. Stir in the salt and pepper. Add the cooked onions and amaranth and stir until thoroughly combined.

Spoon the mixture into the onion halves, allowing any excess filling to spill over into the pan around the onions. Bake uncovered for 1 hour, until brown and bubbly.

Per serving: calories: 286, protein: 14 g, fat: 3 g, carbohydrate: 42 g, fiber: 12 g, sodium: 202 mg

8

Side Dishes

CHAPTER 8: *Side Dishes*

Bangkok Asparagus

YIELD: *6 servings*

This simple Thai-style stir-fried asparagus is a tasty side dish that complements any Asian-inspired meal.

1 pound asparagus
1 tablespoons extra-virgin olive oil
1 large clove garlic, minced or pressed
½ to 1 teaspoon grated fresh ginger

Break off and discard the tough ends of the asparagus. Cut the spears into 1-inch slices on the diagonal.

Heat the oil in a wok or large, heavy skillet over high heat. When a drop of water added to the skillet sizzles, the skillet is ready to use. Add the garlic and ginger and cook and stir for 10 seconds. Add the asparagus and cook and stir for about 2 minutes, or until bright green and tender. Serve immediately.

Per serving: calories: 37, protein: 2 g, fat: 2 g, carbohydrate: 2 g, fiber: 2 g, sodium: 2 mg

Bangkok Asparagus with Toasted Sesame Seeds: Garnish the cooked asparagus with 1 tablespoon of toasted sesame seeds. To toast the sesame seeds, put them in a dry skillet over medium-high heat. Cook, stirring constantly, for 1 to 2 minutes, or until fragrant and slightly golden.

Bangkok Vegetables: Use different vegetables, such as broccoli, carrots, green beans, or snow peas, in place of or in addition to the asparagus.

Asparagus in Corn Sauce

YIELD: *4 servings*

Elegant asparagus spears are slathered in a hearty, cumin-spiked corn sauce and baked until golden brown for an unusual but delectable side dish.

¾ pound asparagus spears, tough ends trimmed
1½ cups frozen corn kernels, thawed
1 stalk celery, chopped
½ teaspoon ground cumin
Salt and ground black pepper

Preheat the oven to 350 degrees F. Lightly mist a loaf pan with nonstick cooking spray.

Put the asparagus in a steamer basket over simmering water. Steam for 4 minutes, or until bright green and crisp-tender. Transfer the asparagus to the loaf pan and reserve the remaining steaming water.

Combine the corn, celery, cumin, and ⅓ cup of the reserved steaming water in a blender. Process until smooth, gradually adding more of the reserved steaming water (up to an additional ⅓ cup) to achieve a pourable consistency. Season with salt and pepper to taste.

Pour the corn sauce over the asparagus. Bake for 30 to 35 minutes, or until golden brown. Serve immediately.

Per serving: calories: 67, protein: 4 g, fat: 0 g, carbohydrate: 12 g, fiber: 3 g, sodium: 14 mg

Lemon-Dill Beets

YIELD: *4 servings*

In this side dish, freshly squeezed lemon juice and chopped dill bring out the vibrant flavor of beets, with just a tad of extra-virgin olive oil and salt and pepper to heighten the taste. Serve warm, cold, or at room temperature.

8 small or 4 large beets, peeled and cut into ½-inch chunks
3 tablespoons freshly squeezed lemon juice
3 tablespoons minced fresh dill, or 1 tablespoon dried dill weed
2 tablespoons extra-virgin olive oil
Salt and ground black pepper

Put the beets in a steamer basket over simmering water. Steam for 15 to 20 minutes, or until fork-tender. Combine the lemon juice, dill, and oil in a large bowl and whisk until thoroughly combined. Add the beets and stir gently until evenly coated. Season with salt and peper to taste. Serve immediately, or transfer to a storage container and refrigerate until ready to serve.

Per serving: calories: 137, protein: 3 g, fat: 7 g, carbohydrate: 14 g, fiber: 3 g, sodium: 131 mg

Pickled Beets

YIELD: *2 cups*

Plan ahead for this recipe, since you have to consume the entire contents of a jar of pickles before you can make it. (It's a tough job, but somebody's got to do it.) Once you have a jar of pickle juice, it couldn't be easier. Simply slice the beets, steam them, and stuff them into the jar. One week later—voila!

3 to 4 beets, peeled, cut in half, and sliced into half-moons (about 1 ⅔ cups)
1 jar (16 ounces) dill pickle juice left over from your favorite pickles (see tip)

Put the beets in a steamer basket over simmering water. Steam for 10 to 15 minutes, or until fork-tender. Transfer the beets to the jar of pickle juice. You may have to stuff the last few in. Make sure that all of the beets are covered with the pickle juice. Seal tightly and refrigerate for 1 week.

Per serving: calories: 26, protein: 1 g, fat: 0 g, carbohydrate: 4 g, fiber: 1 g, sodium: 36 mg

Tip: Use a high-quality, organic brand of dill pickles for this recipe. Those containing unwholesome ingredients, such as corn syrup and artificial coloring, will yield low-quality pickled beets.

Dilly Beans: Replace the steamed beets with 3/4 pound of raw green beans, trimmed (about 70 green beans). Stand them up in the jar of dill pickle juice, seal tightly, and refrigerate for at least 2 weeks.

Roasted Green Beans Almondine

YIELD: *4 to 6 servings*

Veering from convention, the green beans in this dish are roasted rather than boiled or steamed, offering an interesting twist on this culinary favorite. Two pounds of green beans might seem like a lot, but because both trimming and roasting cause shrinkage, the final quantity is just right.

2 pounds green beans, trimmed
4 teaspoons extra-virgin olive oil
Salt and ground black pepper
⅓ cup slivered almonds, toasted (see tip)

Preheat the oven to 400 degrees F. Mist a baking sheet with nonstick cooking spray.

Put the green beans in a large bowl. Drizzle with the oil and sprinkle with salt and pepper. Toss gently to coat. Arrange the beans in a single layer on the prepared baking sheet. Roast in the oven for about 30 minutes, or until slightly blistered and browned.

Transfer to a serving platter. Sprinkle the almonds over the beans and serve immediately.

Per serving: calories: 139, protein: 5 g, fat: 8 g, carbohydrate: 7 g, fiber: 7 g, sodium: 12 mg

Tip: To toast slivered almonds, put them in a dry skillet over medium-high heat. Cook, stirring constantly, for about 4 minutes, or until aromatic and slightly golden.

Green Bean Casserole

YIELD: *4 servings*

Remember old-fashioned green bean casserole made with condensed mushroom soup and fried onion rings? This updated version abandons the junk food components in favor of more wholesome ingredients—creamy vegan mushroom soup and fresh onions.

1 large onion, cut in half and sliced into thin half-moons
1 tablespoon extra-virgin olive oil
½ teaspoon salt
1½ pounds fresh green beans, trimmed and cut into 1-inch lengths,
    or 1 package (16 ounces) frozen cut green beans
1 cup store-bought creamy vegan mushroom soup
1 cup shredded vegan cheese
Ground black pepper

Position an oven rack several inches under the broiler and preheat the broiler. Lightly mist a baking sheet with nonstick cooking spray.

Combine the onion, oil, and salt in a medium bowl and toss until evenly coated. Arrange the onion in a single layer on the prepared baking sheet and broil for about 7 minutes, or until brown. Flip or stir the onion and broil for about 5 more minutes, or until browned. Remove from the oven and lower the oven temperature to 350 degrees F.

If using frozen green beans, cook them according to the package directions. If using fresh green beans, put them in a steamer basket over simmering water. Steam for about 10 minutes, or until tender. Combine the beans and onion in a large bowl. Add the soup, vegan cheese, and pepper to taste. Stir gently until thoroughly combined.

Transfer the mixture to an unoiled 8-inch square baking pan. Bake for about 30 minutes, or until bubbly.

Per serving: calories: 209, protein: 5 g, fat: 11 g, carbohydrate: 19 g, fiber: 8 g, sodium: 636 mg

Roasted Brussels Sprouts with Toasted Pine Nuts
YIELD: *4 servings*

Even those who don't normally like brussels sprouts will be won over by their satisfying, earthy flavor when they are roasted. In this recipe, they are elevated to a sophisticated side dish with the addition of toasted pine nuts for delicate flavor and crunch.

1 pound brussels sprouts, trimmed and cut in half vertically
2 to 4 cloves garlic, minced or pressed
4 teaspoons extra-virgin olive oil
1 tablespoon balsamic vinegar
Salt and ground black pepper
2 tablespoons pine nuts, toasted (see tip)

Preheat the oven to 450 degrees F. Lightly mist a baking sheet with nonstick cooking spray.

Put the brussels sprouts and garlic in a large bowl. Drizzle with the oil and vinegar and sprinkle with salt and pepper. Toss until evenly coated. Arrange the brussels sprouts in a single layer on the prepared baking sheet. Roast for 20 to 30 minutes, or until the brussels sprouts are fork-tender and the outer leaves are browned.

Toss with the toasted pine nuts and serve immediately.

Per serving: calories: 127, protein: 5 g, fat: 8 g, carbohydrate: 8 g, fiber: 5 g, sodium: 33 mg

Tip: To toast pine nuts, put them in a dry skillet over medium-high heat. Cook, stirring constantly, for 1 to 2 minutes, or until fragrant and slightly golden.

Purple Cabbage with Sesame Sauce

YIELD: *4 servings*

Steamed purple cabbage is tossed with a rich and creamy blend of tahini and miso in this simple but amazingly flavorful dish. It's such a delicious way to prepare cabbage that this humble but healthful vegetable may soon become a staple in your shopping cart.

1 purple cabbage, coarsely chopped
⅓ cup tahini
¼ cup hot water
2½ tablespoons dark miso
Ground black pepper

Put the cabbage in a steamer basket over simmering water. Steam for about 10 minutes, or until tender.

Meanwhile, combine the tahini, water, and miso in a small bowl. Stir until smooth. Transfer the cabbage to a large bowl. Immediately add the tahini sauce and mix well. (Don't let the cabbage get too cool before adding the sauce; it must be moist and steamy for optimal flavor and texture.) Sprinkle generously with pepper and serve immediately.

Per serving: calories: 161, protein: 7 g, fat: 10 g, carbohydrate: 10 g, fiber: 5 g, sodium: 417 mg

Double Sesame Cabbage: Stir in 1 tablespoon of sesame seeds along with the pepper.

Crispy Artichoke Hearts

YIELD: *4 servings*

People will be impressed with your culinary prowess when you serve these fabulous yet easy-to-prepare artichoke hearts. They make a great appetizer and will be even more of a hit when accompanied by Agave-Mustard Dipping Sauce (page 63), Creamy Dijon Dipping Sauce (page 64), or Creamy Horseradish Dipping Sauce (page 62), though plain vegan mayonnaise will do in a pinch.

¾ cup unbleached flour
1 tablespoon garlic powder
¼ teaspoon salt
⅛ teaspoon ground black pepper
2 cans (15 ounces each) artichoke hearts, drained
4 tablespoons vegetable oil, or as needed

Combine the flour, garlic powder, salt, and pepper in an 8-inch square baking pan. Whisk until thoroughly combined. Arrange half of the artichoke hearts in a single layer over the flour mixture. Gently shake the pan back and forth to roll the artichokes around and coat them with the flour mixture. You may have to turn some of them by hand to coat them on all sides.

Heat 2 tablespoons of the oil in a large nonstick skillet over medium-high heat. When a drop of water added to the skillet sizzles, the oil is hot enough for the artichokes. One by one, gently shake the excess flour off the artichokes and carefully place them in the skillet, keeping 1 inch between them. (Depending on the size of your skillet, you may need to cook the artichokes in two batches.) Cook for about 2 minutes, until the artichokes start to brown. Carefully turn the artichokes using tongs. Continue cooking and turning the artichokes until they are light brown and crispy all over.

Transfer to a wire rack to drain off any excess oil. If you are cooking the artichokes in two batches, wipe out the skillet with a paper towel. Pour in the remaining 2 tablespoons of vegetable oil and repeat the cooking process with the remaining artichokes. Serve immediately.

Per serving: calories: 285, protein: 7 g, fat: 14 g, carbohydrate: 31 g, fiber: 3 g, sodium: 757 mg

Harvest Mash

YIELD: *4 servings*

Traditional mashed potatoes get a vibrant and flavorful makeover with the addi-tion of yam, carrots, and cabbage. Both green and purple cabbage taste great in this dish, but purple cabbage will impart a lovely reddish hue. In addition to enjoying the mash as is, you can transform it into a casserole or patties as described in the variations.

4 cups water or vegetable broth
3 large white potatoes, chopped
1½ cups chopped green or purple cabbage
1 small yam, peeled and chopped
2 carrots, chopped

Put all of the ingredients in a large soup pot. Bring to a boil over high heat. Turn the heat down to medium-low, cover, and cook for about 40 minutes, or until all of the vegetables are tender.

Drain, reserving the cooking liquid, and return the vegetables to the pot or transfer them to a large bowl. Mash the vegetables, stirring in up to half of the reserved cooking liquid to reach the desired consistency. (If you like, you can use the remaining cooking liquid as a broth in another dish.)

Per serving: calories: 281, protein: 6 g, fat: 0 g, carbohydrate: 62 g, fiber: 8 g, sodium: 48 mg

Harvest Mash Casserole: Spoon the Harvest Mash into a lightly oiled loaf pan, gently packing it in and smoothing the top with the back of the spoon. Use a fork to make furrows on the surface. Broil for about 5 minutes, or until the top turns golden brown.

Harvest Mash Patties: Refrigerate the prepared Harvest Mash for at least 2 hours. Put ½ cup of breadcrumbs in a flat-bottomed bowl. Stir in 2 tablespoons of sesame seeds and 2 teaspoons of dried dill weed. Shape ⅓ cup of the cold Harvest Mash into a ball and roll it in the breadcrumbs, pressing gently to work some of the crumbs into the ball. Roll the ball in the mixture again until completely covered with crumbs. Press the ball into a patty and set aside on parchment paper. Repeat with the remaining Harvest Mash. Fry the patties in a lightly oiled skillet over medium-high heat for 3 to 5 minutes per side. Serve as is or on buns with lettuce, tomato, and whatever condiments and other accompaniments you like.

Smashed and Spiked Potatoes

YIELD: *4 to 6 servings*

Mashed potatoes provide the perfect cover for white beans, creating a great opportunity to add a hearty dose of fiber and complex carbohydrates to the diet of even confirmed "legumophobes." Roasted garlic adds a warm, mellow flavor that makes this dish memorable.

4 white potatoes, scrubbed and cut into large chunks
1 can (15 ounces) white beans (such as cannellini beans or great northern beans),
    rinsed and drained
¼ cup plus 3 tablespoons water
3 tablespoons extra-virgin olive oil
1 head roasted garlic (see tip), mashed, or ½ teaspoon garlic powder
Salt and ground black pepper

Fill a large saucepan halfway with water and bring to a boil over high heat. Add the potatoes and cook for 10 to 15 minutes, or until fork-tender. Drain the potatoes and return them to the saucepan or transfer them to a large bowl.

Combine the beans, water, and oil in a food processor. Pulse 6 times, or until the beans are coarsely chopped. Add the bean mixture and garlic to the potatoes and mash or mix to achieve the desired consistency. Season with salt and pepper to taste before serving.

Per serving: calories: 278, protein: 10 g, fat: 8 g, carbohydrate: 40 g, fiber: 6 g, sodium: 11 mg

Tip: To roast the garlic, preheat the oven to 400 degrees F. Remove the loose, outer layers of papery skin from one head of garlic, leaving just enough to hold all of the cloves together. Cut off the tips of the individual cloves so that you can see the fresh garlic within. Place the whole head on a piece of aluminum foil and drizzle 1 tablespoon of extra-virgin olive oil over the top. Wrap the foil around the garlic and seal completely. Place the package in a small baking dish (in case any olive oil escapes) and bake for 40 minutes, or until the garlic is soft and lightly browned. Cool the garlic slightly, then use a knife or fork to remove the garlic cloves from their paper casings. Alternatively, simply squeeze the bottom of the garlic head over a bowl so that all of the garlic shoots out at once.

Kid-Style Mashed Potatoes: Peel the potatoes before boiling. When processing the beans, replace the water with unsweetened nondairy milk, omit the olive oil and garlic, and process until the beans are completely smooth. Mash the potatoes with 1 tablespoon of nonhydrogenated vegan margarine before stirring in the bean mixture.

Rosemary Sweet Potatoes

YIELD: *4 servings*

These sweet potatoes, roasted with a sprinkling of extra-virgin olive oil, salt, and fresh rosemary, are sophisticated, scrumptious, and beautiful, not to mention a real crowd-pleaser.

2 large sweet potatoes or yams, peeled or unpeeled and cut into ¾-inch chunks
2 tablespoons extra-virgin olive oil
2 tablespoons minced fresh rosemary
¾ teaspoon salt

Preheat the oven to 450 degrees F. Mist a baking sheet with nonstick cooking spray.

Put the sweet potatoes in a large bowl. Sprinkle with the oil, rosemary, and salt. Toss until evenly coated. Arrange the sweet potatoes in a single layer on the prepared baking sheet. Roast in the oven for about 25 minutes, or until fork-tender.

Per serving: calories: 163, protein: 2 g, fat: 7 g, carbohydrate: 20 g, fiber: 4 g, sodium: 441 mg

Sweet Potatoes with Cranberries, Apricots, and Pecans

YIELD: *6 servings*

The brilliant colors in this festive side dish make it an ideal complement to any autumn or winter meal, especially during the holiday season.

4 sweet potatoes, peeled and chopped
½ pound fresh cranberries
½ cup pecans, finely chopped
8 dried apricots, finely chopped

Preheat the oven to 350 degrees F. Lightly mist an 8 x 11-inch baking dish or a casserole dish of similar size with nonstick cooking spray.

Put the sweet potatoes and cranberries in the prepared baking dish and mix well. Add the pecans and apricots. Stir just a bit so that the pecans and apricots stay near the top of the mixture. Cover and bake for about 1 hour, or until the sweet potatoes are tender.

Per serving: calories: 355, protein: 6 g, fat: 7 g, carbohydrate: 58 g, fiber: 12 g, sodium: 90 mg

Purple Sweet Potato Pie

YIELD: *4 servings*

If you have yet to discover purple sweet potatoes, you're in for a pleasant surprise. Not only do they retain their gorgeous color when cooked, they actually take on an even richer, deeper hue, making this pie a beautiful sight to behold. If purple sweet potatoes aren't available, use regular sweet potatoes instead, adding a piece of beet for extra color if you like.

3 large purple sweet potatoes, peeled and chopped
2 cups water
4 cups chopped leafy green vegetables (such as bok choy,
    collard greens, kale, or spinach)
3 tablespoons light miso
1 (9-inch) whole-grain vegan pie crust

Combine the potatoes and water in a large pot over high heat and bring to a boil. Turn the heat down to medium-low and cook, stirring occasionally, for about 20 minutes, or until tender. Add the leafy greens and cook for 1 minute, or until the greens are bright green and wilted. Drain, reserving the cooking water, and return the vegetables to the pot or transfer them to a large bowl.

Preheat the oven to 350 degrees F.

Combine the miso and 3 tablespoons of the reserved cooking water in a small bowl. Stir until thoroughly combined. Add the miso to the cooked vegetables. Mash until the desired consistency is achieved, gradually adding up to ½ cup of the remaining cooking water as needed.

Spoon the mixture into the pie crust, gently packing it down with the back of a spoon and creating a dome shape that rises above the crust. Bake for about 50 minutes, or until the crust turns golden brown.

Per serving: calories: 452, protein: 8 g, fat: 16 g, carbohydrate: 60 g, fiber: 8 g, sodium: 994 mg

Broccoli-Rice Casserole

YIELD: *4 servings*

This recipe, made with store-bought creamy vegan broccoli soup and vegan cheese, is soothing and delicious—a must for anyone who loves comfort food. You'll earn extra popularity points if you bring it to a potluck or offer it as a festive holiday side dish. It's particularly good when served as leftovers the next day—but good luck with having any left over!

3 cups water
1½ cups short-grain brown rice
4 cups bite-size broccoli florets, or 1 package (10 ounces)
    frozen broccoli, thawed and drained well
2 cups creamy vegan broccoli soup
1½ cups shredded vegan cheddar cheese
Salt and ground black pepper

Combine the water and rice in a medium saucepan over high heat and bring to a boil. Turn the heat down to low, cover, and cook for about 50 minutes, or until the water is absorbed. Transfer the rice to a large bowl.

Preheat the oven to 350 degrees F.

If using fresh broccoli, put it in a steamer basket over simmering water. Steam for about 5 minutes, or until bright green and crisp-tender. If using frozen broccoli, make sure it's completely thawed and drained. Add the broccoli, soup, and vegan cheese to the rice and stir well. Season with salt and pepper to taste.

Transfer the mixture to an unoiled 8 x 12-inch baking dish or a casserole dish of similar size. Bake for about 45 minutes, or until bubbly and lightly browned. Let sit for at least 10 minutes before serving.

Per serving: calories: 455, protein: 13 g, fat: 14 g, carbohydrate: 72 g, fiber: 8 g, sodium: 604 mg

Polenta Provençal

YIELD: *9 servings*

Infused with sundried tomatoes and fresh basil, this colorful polenta is gorgeous, making it a particularly appropriate side dish when you have company for dinner. Just be prepared to be patient. Polenta takes more than half an hour to cook, and you have to stir it the whole time. Try to enjoy the moment and maintain positive, loving thoughts while you stir and stir and stir; polenta tastes best when you do it that way.

1 jar (8.5 ounces) chopped sundried tomatoes packed in oil (see tip)
6 cups water
2 teaspoons salt, plus more as needed
1 cup coarse or medium-ground corn grits
¼ cup chopped fresh basil
Ground black pepper

Lightly mist an 8-inch square baking pan with nonstick cooking spray.

Drain the sundried tomatoes (reserve the oil for use in salad dressing or another recipe). Pour 3 cups of the water into a medium saucepan over medium-high heat and bring to a simmer. Lower the heat, cover, and keep it simmering for use later in the recipe.

Combine the remaining 3 cups of water and 2 teaspoons of the salt in a large, heavy saucepan over medium-high heat. Bring to a boil. While whisking continuously in a circular motion, slowly pour the grits into the middle of the pan in a steady stream. Lower the heat to maintain a gentle simmer and continue whisking constantly. When the mixture begins to thicken, switch from using a whisk to a wooden spoon and, still stirring constantly, add 1 cup of the simmering water. Continue stirring constantly.

After 7 to 10 minutes, or when the mixture gets very thick again, add another cup of the simmering water. Continue to stir until it gets thick again. Add the remaining simmering water and keep stirring for 5 to 10 minutes, or until the mixture thickens. Stir in the tomatoes and basil and continue cooking, stirring constantly, for 5 more minutes. Remove from the heat. Season with additional salt, if needed, and pepper to taste.

Transfer the polenta to the prepared pan, smoothing the surface with the back of a spoon. Cool to room temperature; then refrigerate for 30 minutes. Cut into 9 squares. Serve at room temperature. Alternatively, position an oven rack several inches below the broiler and preheat the broiler. Arrange the squares on a baking sheet and broil for about 5 minutes, or until browned.

Per serving: calories: 106, protein: 2 g, fat: 4 g, carbohydrate: 14 g, fiber: 3 g, sodium: 550 mg

Tip: If chopped sundried tomatoes are not available, use whole sundried tomatoes (packed in oil) and coarsely chop them.

Creamy Millet Casserole

YIELD: *3 servings*

Cooked millet can have a grainy texture, but when it is baked with a rich and velvety soup, it becomes soft and creamy. Consider this casserole a delicious and convenient way to add variety to your dinner plate.

3 cups water
1 cup millet
2 cups cut fresh green beans, in ¾-inch lengths, or 1 package (10 ounces)
    frozen cut green beans, thawed (see tip)
1 cup shredded vegan cheese
1 cup store-bought creamy vegan corn soup
Salt and ground black pepper

Bring the water to a boil in a small saucepan over medium-high heat. Add the millet and stir well. Return to a boil. Turn the heat down to low, cover, and cook for about 25 minutes, or until the water is absorbed. Transfer the millet to a large bowl.

Preheat the oven to 350 degrees F. Mist an 8 x 11-inch baking pan with non-stick cooking spray.

If using fresh green beans, put them in a steamer basket over simmering water. Steam for about 7 minutes, or until crisp-tender. If using frozen green beans, make sure they're completely thawed and drained. Add the green beans, cheese, and soup to the millet and stir well. Season with salt and pepper to taste.

Transfer the mixture to the prepared pan and smooth the top with the back of a spoon. Bake for about 25 minutes, or until bubbly and lightly browned. Serve immediately.

Per serving: calories: 435, protein: 11 g, fat: 12 g, carbohydrate: 67 g, fiber: 7 g, sodium: 539 mg

Tip: If using frozen green beans, put them in a bowl of warm water while the millet is cooking. Once they're thawed, let them sit in a colander for 5 to 10 minutes to drain off the excess water.

Sweet-and-Tangy Chickpeas

YIELD: *4 servings*

Made in the spirit of baked beans, these delicious chickpeas are a great summer-time side dish. They can even be the main course when served with potatoes or brown rice.

2 cans (15 ounces each) chickpeas, rinsed and drained
1 can (8 ounces) tomato sauce
½ cup agave nectar
1 small onion, finely chopped

Preheat the oven to 350 degrees F.

Combine all of the ingredients in an 8-inch square baking dish or a casserole dish of similar size. Stir well. Cover and bake for about 1 hour, or until bubbly. Let sit for 5 minutes before serving.

Per serving: calories: 342, protein: 12 g, fat: 3 g, carbohydrate: 68 g, fiber: 10 g, sodium: 157 mg

Middle Eastern Fava Beans

YIELD: *4 servings*

Tahini lends Middle Eastern flavor to fava beans in this interesting side dish. It can easily be converted to a main dish; just serve it with rice and a salad of marinated cucumbers, tomatoes, onion, and parsley. If you can't find fava beans, it's fine to substitute pinto beans.

6 tablespoons tahini
2 tablespoons freshly squeezed lemon juice
3 cloves garlic, minced
½ cup plus 2 tablespoons water
2 cans (15 ounces each) fava beans, rinsed and drained

Preheat the oven to 350 degrees F.

Put the tahini, lemon juice, and garlic in a medium bowl. Gradually add the water, whisking until thoroughly combined. Add the beans and stir until evenly coated.

Transfer the mixture to a 9-inch square baking dish or a casserole dish of similar size. Cover and bake for about 30 minutes, or until bubbly, stirring the beans after 15 minutes. Serve immediately, as the mixture will thicken once it starts to cool.

Per serving: calories: 368, protein: 20 g, fat: 12 g, carbohydrate: 35 g, fiber: 13 g, sodium: 28 mg

Cuban Black Beans

YIELD: *4 to 6 servings*

Don't let the simplicity of this recipe fool you. Oregano, onion powder, and red wine vinegar transform a simple can of black beans into what some might consider restaurant fare. This dish is excellent served over brown basmati rice.

2 cans (15 ounces each) black beans, undrained
2 teaspoons red wine vinegar
2 teaspoons dried oregano
1 teaspoon onion powder
½ teaspoon salt

Combine all of the ingredients in a medium saucepan and mix well. Bring to a boil over medium-high heat. Turn the heat down to low and cook, stirring occasionally, for 5 to 10 minutes.

Per serving: calories: 131, protein: 9 g, fat: 0 g, carbohydrate: 24 g, fiber: 8 g, sodium: 233 mg

9

Desserts, Treats, and Sweet Toppings

CHAPTER 9: *Desserts, Treats, and Sweet Toppings*

Melon Balls in Mint Liqueur

YIELD: *4 servings*

Fruit soaked in liqueur is a simple but elegant dessert. I've upped the exotic factor by drizzling melon balls with mint liqueur and garnishing them with chocolate shavings and shredded coconut. Feel free to substitute any fruit liqueur for the mint liqueur. For a stunning visual presentation, serve this dessert in champagne glasses, wine glasses, or fancy glass dessert dishes.

1 cantaloupe, cut in half and seeded
1 to 2 tablespoons mint liqueur
2 tablespoons shaved chocolate, for garnish (see tip)
1 tablespoon unsweetened shredded dried coconut, for garnish

Use the smaller end of a melon baller to scoop out balls of cantaloupe. Put the melon balls in a medium bowl. Drizzle with the liqueur and gently stir until evenly coated. Let sit for 10 minutes.

Divide the melon balls evenly among 4 serving dishes. Sprinkle with the chocolate and coconut. Serve immediately.

Per serving: calories: 159, protein: 2 g, fat: 7 g, carbohydrate: 20 g, fiber: 2 g, sodium: 23 mg

Tip: According to Diane Wagemann, chocolatier extraordinaire from the vegan oasis Divine Treasures Chocolates, in Manchester, Connecticut, it's easy to make shaved chocolate at home. Here's how to do it: Refrigerate a vegan chocolate bar for at least 1 hour. Remove the wrapper and hold the chocolate bar with a paper towel. Using a vegetable peeler, peel or shave a narrow end of the chocolate bar. The chocolate will curl up like wood shavings.

Hot Spiced Apples

YIELD: *2 servings*

Simmered dates add just enough sweetness to keep these succulent apples on the healthful side, and cinnamon and cloves provide tried-and-true flavoring. This cozy dessert is nourishing enough to eat for breakfast. Or turn up the decadence factor by topping it with a scoop of vegan vanilla ice cream.

⅔ cup water
4 pitted medjool dates, chopped
6 whole cloves
2 tart and crisp red apples (such as Fuji), cut into bite-size chunks
½ teaspoon ground cinnamon

Put the water, dates, and cloves in a small saucepan. Bring to a simmer over medium-high heat. Turn the heat down to low, cover, and cook for 5 minutes. Stir in the apples and cinnamon. Cook, covered, for about 7 minutes, or until the apples are soft. Remove the cloves and serve immediately.

Per serving: calories: 127, protein: 1 g, fat: 1 g, carbohydrate: 28 g, fiber: 5 g, sodium: 1 mg

Divine Baked Pears

YIELD: *4 to 8 servings*

This pretty dish is a light and sophisticated dessert for a special dinner party. Do the prep in advance but wait until right before you start eating dinner to pop the pears in the oven. As dinner winds down, a heavenly aroma will inform you and your guests that it is indeed time for dessert. For an extra-special presentation, serve each pear topped with a scoop of vegan vanilla ice cream or another light-flavored vegan ice cream.

½ cup water
4 firm pears
½ cup dried fruit in small pieces (such as raisins, dried cherries, dried cranberries, chopped dates, or a combination)
½ cup maple syrup
½ teaspoon ground cinnamon

Preheat the oven to 375 degrees F. Lightly mist an 8 x 11-inch baking pan with nonstick cooking spray; then pour in the water.

Slice the pears in half lengthwise. Scoop out the seeds (a melon baller works well), and if desired, slice off the very top portion of the pear, including the stem. Place the pears cut-side up in the pan, arranging them so they don't tilt too much. Fill the pear cavities with the dried fruit.

Combine the maple syrup and the cinnamon in a small bowl and mix well. Drizzle the syrup over the top surface of the pears, including over the dried fruit.

Cover with foil and bake for about 1 hour, or until the pears are very soft. Cool for 5 minutes before serving.

Per serving: calories: 176, protein: 1 g, fat: 1 g, carbohydrate: 42 g, fiber: 3 g, sodium: 4 mg

Pear-fect Strudel

YIELD: *6 servings*

This autumn-inspired dessert can do double duty as a special weekend breakfast. Pears and apricots are so flavorful that no additional sweetener is needed in this aromatic dish. For a special treat, top the strudel with vegan vanilla ice cream.

2 large Bartlett pears, cored and chopped
15 dried apricots, chopped
½ teaspoon pumpkin pie spice
8 sheets phyllo dough
3 tablespoons extra-virgin olive oil, or as needed

Put the pears in a medium saucepan and mash a few of the pieces to make just enough juice to cover the bottom of pan. (This prevents sticking.) Stir in the apricots and pumpkin pie spice. Cook over medium-high heat, stirring frequently, for 5 to 10 minutes, or until the moisture has evaporated. Remove from the heat before the mixture starts to stick. It should have the consistency of chunky fruit jelly.

Preheat the oven to 350 degrees F. Lightly mist an 8-inch square baking pan with nonstick cooking spray.

Place a sheet of phyllo dough in the bottom of the prepared pan, allowing the excess to drape over the edge, and brush it with a light coating of the oil. Repeat this layering process for a total of 8 sheets of phyllo dough.

Spoon the pear filling into the center of the pan, spreading it no closer than 1 inch from the edges of the phyllo dough. Wrap the overhanging edges of the top sheet of phyllo dough over the pear mixture and tuck them into the pan. Brush the top with a light coating of the oil. Repeat with remaining overhanging edges, sheet by sheet, brushing each layer with the oil. Be sure to tuck the edges of the final sheet all the way over the mixture.

Bake for about 20 minutes, or until the top is golden brown and flaky. Serve warm or cooled.

Per serving: calories: 210, protein: 4 g, fat: 8 g, carbohydrate: 32 g, fiber: 4 g, sodium: 101 mg

Berry Turnovers

YIELD: *about 10 turnovers*

In these turnovers, the naturally wonderful flavor of berries is heightened with agave nectar. The amazing aroma wafting from your oven may make you extremely eager to tuck into this wonderful dessert. Be sure to slow down and savor every bite.

1 cup plus 1 tablespoon whole wheat pastry flour
¼ teaspoon salt
¼ cup extra-virgin olive oil
3 tablespoons cold water
1 cup mixed fresh or frozen berries (such as blackberries, blueberries, or raspberries)
¼ cup agave nectar
⅛ teaspoon ground cinnamon

Put 1 cup of the flour and the salt in a medium bowl and whisk to combine. Combine the oil and water in a separate small bowl. Whisk until emulsified. To make the dough, pour the oil mixture into the flour mixture. Stir with a sturdy spoon until thoroughly combined, but don't overstir or the dough will be tough.

Transfer the dough to a lightly floured surface. Form the dough into a ball. Roll it out to a thickness of about ¼ inch. Cut the dough into circles about 3 inches in diameter using a cookie cutter or the rim of a large glass. Gently form the scraps into a ball, roll it out, and cut it into more circles. You should have about 10 circles in all.

Preheat the oven to 375 degrees F. Lightly mist a baking sheet with nonstick cooking spray and set aside.

Put the berries, agave nectar, cinnamon, and the remaining 1 tablespoon of flour in a medium bowl. Stir until thoroughly combined. Place 1 heaping tablespoon of the berry filling in the center of a dough circle. Fold the dough in half over the berries. Pinch the edges to seal. Repeat with the remaining dough and filling. Carefully transfer to the prepared baking sheet.

Bake for about 20 minutes, or until golden brown.

Per turnover: calories: 121, protein: 2 g, fat: 6 g, carbohydrate: 15 g, fiber: 2 g, sodium: 54 mg

Berry Tartlets: Prepare the dough circles and filling as directed. Lightly mist 10 muffin cups with nonstick cooking spray. Line the muffin cups with the dough. Fill each cup with 1 tablespoon of the filling. Bake as directed.

Banana, Chocolate, and Ginger Pastry

YIELD: *16 pieces*

For a divine dessert that's also fairly healthful, satisfy your chocolate cravings with this ginger-kissed dessert.

6 bananas, coarsely chopped
3 cups vegan chocolate chips
⅔ cup crystallized ginger, finely chopped
8 sheets phyllo dough
3 tablespoons extra-virgin olive oil, or as needed

Preheat the oven to 350 degrees F. Lightly mist an 8-inch square baking pan with nonstick cooking spray.

Combine the bananas, chocolate chips, and ginger in a large bowl and mix well.

Place a sheet of phyllo dough in the bottom of the prepared pan, allowing the excess to drape over the edges, and brush with a light coating of the oil. Repeat this layering process for a total of 4 sheets of phyllo dough.

Spread the banana mixture over the phyllo dough and gently flatten the top using the back of a spoon. Lay a sheet of phyllo dough over the filling, allowing the excess to drape over the edge, and brush with a light coating of oil. Repeat with the remaining phyllo dough for a total of 4 sheets on top of the filling.

Wrap the overhanging edges of the phyllo dough over the top layer and tuck them into the pan. Brush the top with a light coating of oil.

Bake for about 30 minutes, or until the top is flaky and golden brown. Cut into 16 squares and serve warm.

Per piece: calories: 276, protein: 3 g, fat: 12 g, carbohydrate: 39 g, fiber: 2 g, sodium: 43 mg

Strawberry Chocolate Crisps

YIELD: *4 servings*

In this light and fruity recipe, rice cakes are spread with a mixture of strawberries and dates, topped with chocolate chips, and baked until the chocolate melts. It's sinfully good.

8 ounces strawberries, hulled and chopped
10 pitted dates, chopped
4 rice cakes, plain or lightly salted
¼ cup vegan chocolate chips

Put the strawberries in a small saucepan and mash a few of them to create a few tablespoons of liquid on the bottom of the pan. Stir in the dates. Cook over medium-high heat, stirring frequently, for 5 to 10 minutes, or until the dates are very soft. Mash the dates and strawberries, leaving the mixture a bit lumpy. Remove from the heat and let cool to thicken.

Preheat the oven to 350 degrees F.

Place the rice cakes on a baking sheet. Spread the strawberry mixture on top of the rice cakes. Top with the chocolate chips. Bake for about 10 minutes, or until the chocolate chips melt and the rice cakes start to turn golden brown at the edges. Serve immediately.

Per serving: calories: 165, protein: 2 g, fat: 3 g, carbohydrate: 31 g, fiber: 3 g, sodium: 5 mg

Chocolate-Covered Strawberries

YIELD: *12 strawberries*

Valentine's Day comes but once a year, but that's no reason to abstain from dipping strawberries in chocolate all summer long. The next time a chocoholic friend or loved one has a birthday or some other reason to celebrate, consider presenting a dozen chocolate-covered strawberries in a pretty box. Although it won't be expensive, it will be extravagant and sure to please.

1½ cups vegan chocolate chips
12 large strawberries (with the leaves intact), washed and thoroughly dried

Line a baking sheet with parchment paper.

Pour about 2 inches of water into a large skillet. Bring to a simmer over medium heat. Put the chocolate chips in a heatproof bowl or saucepan. Set the bowl in the simmering water. Stir the chocolate chips for about 5 minutes, until melted and completely smooth.

Transfer the entire setup (the skillet with the hot water and the bowl of chocolate) to a heatproof surface. Grasping the leaves, dip the pointed end of a strawberry into the melted chocolate, rolling it around a bit to cover all but the top ¼-inch. Lay the strawberry on the prepared pan. Repeat with the remaining strawberries.

Refrigerate the strawberries for at least 15 minutes. To store Chocolate-Covered Strawberries, arrange them in a single layer in storage containers and refrigerate until serving time.

Per strawberry: calories: 114, protein: 1 g, fat: 6 g, carbohydrate: 14 g, fiber: 1 g, sodium: 0 mg

Tip: You may have a bit of melted chocolate left over after dipping the strawberries. Don't despair! (As if!) Use the extra however you wish: dip a few extra strawberries (or anything you like) in it, add it to a smoothie, or drizzle it over a dessert.

Chocolate-Covered Potato Chips: To prepare this rather decadent sweet-and-salty snack, replace the strawberries with about 20 thick potato chips.

Chocolate-Covered Pretzels: Replace the strawberries with either 12 large pretzels or 2½ cups of small pretzels. If using large pretzels, dip them as you would the strawberries. If using small pretzels, either dip them as you would the strawberries, or put all of them in the bowl of melted chocolate at the same time and stir gently to coat. Remove them in clumps, a spoonful at a time, and transfer to parchment paper to cool.

Vegan Fudge

YIELD: *25 squares*

Your culinary skills will be revered when you serve this mouthwatering vegan fudge. People may imagine that you slaved over the stove all day to create this confection, but the truth is, this recipe is virtually infallible and takes only a few minutes to prepare.

1 package (12 ounces) vegan chocolate chips
1 cup vegan marshmallow crème
½ cup crunchy unsalted peanut butter

Lightly mist an 8-inch square baking pan with nonstick cooking spray.

Pour about 2 inches of water into a large skillet. Bring to a simmer over medium heat. Put the chocolate chips in a heatproof bowl or saucepan. Set the bowl in the simmering water. Stir the chocolate chips for about 5 minutes, until melted and completely smooth.

Transfer the bowl to a heatproof surface. Add the marshmallow créme and peanut butter and stir until thoroughly blended. Transfer the mixture to the prepared pan and smooth out the top with the back of a spoon.

Cool for 15 minutes. Refrigerate, uncovered, for 1 hour. Cover with plastic wrap and refrigerate for at least 2 more hours before cutting into 25 squares.

Per square: calories: 114, protein: 2 g, fat: 6 g, carbohydrate: 12 g, fiber: 1 g, sodium: 3 mg

Almond Fudge: Replace the peanut butter with either smooth or crunchy almond butter.

Fudge Crisp: Add 1 cup of crispy rice cereal to the melted chocolate chips, stirring it in gently but thoroughly. Add the remaining ingredients and proceed as directed.

Chocolate Fondue

YIELD: *2¼ cups*

This rich, velvety sauce is hot and tantalizing. Your fondue pot will be like an oasis surrounded by your favorite dipping items, and everyone will be irresistibly drawn to it. By the way, you don't need a fondue pot to enjoy this recipe. Just serve it in the pot you cooked it in or transfer it to a pretty serving dish. It may not be as glamorous, but no one will care, and chances are quite high that the fondue will be completely consumed before it has a chance to cool.

1 package (12 ounces) vegan chocolate chips
¼ cup plus 1 to 2 tablespoons vanilla nondairy milk
¼ cup vegan marshmallow crème
Optional: 3 tablespoons creamy peanut butter

Pour about 2 inches of water into a large skillet. Bring to a simmer over medium heat. Combine the chocolate chips and ¼ cup of the nondairy milk in a heatproof bowl or saucepan. Set the bowl in the simmering water. Stir the chocolate chips for about 5 minutes, until melted and completely smooth.

Stir in the marshmallow crème and the peanut butter, if using. Stir in the remaining nondairy milk, 1 tablespoon at a time, until the desired consistency is achieved. If you like, transfer the mixture to a fondue pot over low heat.

Per ¼ cup: calories: 210, protein: 2 g, fat: 11 g, carbohydrate: 26 g, fiber: 1 g, sodium: 5 mg

Tip: Serve Chocolate Fondue with fondue skewers and whatever dipping items you like. Good choices for dipping include mixed fruits, such as whole strawberries, orange segments, and thick banana slices; vegan marshmallows; mini pretzels; or cubed vegan pound cake.

Halvah

YIELD: *24 pieces*

Halvah, a traditional Jewish treat, is usually made with sugar or honey. In this updated version, it is sweetened with dates instead of sugar, but it's still just as rich. Enjoy it as a dessert or high-energy snack.

½ cup pitted dates (about 10 dates)
½ cup tahini
½ cup cashew butter
1 teaspoon vanilla extract
Optional: 1 tablespoon agave nectar

Line a loaf pan with a 12 x 12-inch piece of parchment paper, letting the excess drape over the sides of the pan.

Combine the dates, tahini, cashew butter, and vanilla extract in a food processor. Process until almost completely smooth, with just a bit of graininess. Taste the halvah. If you would like it sweeter, add the agave nectar and process for a few more seconds. Press the mixture into the bottom of the prepared pan. Fold the parchment paper over to completely cover the mixture.

Refrigerate for at least 3 hours. Unwrap the halvah and cut it into 24 pieces: 3 cuts widthwise and 5 cuts lengthwise.

Per piece: calories: 70, protein: 2 g, fat: 5 g, carbohydrate: 5 g, fiber: 1 g, sodium: 5 mg

Bliss Balls

YIELD: *about 25 balls*

You can serve this wholesome treat for dessert, but it also makes a great snack food when you're hiking, bicycling, or working outside, or anytime your energy needs are high.

1½ cups raw almonds
⅔ cups pitted medjool dates
3 tablespoons brown rice syrup
2 teaspoons vanilla extract, almond liqueur, or chocolate liqueur

Put the almonds in a food processor. Process until coarsely ground. Add the dates, rice syrup, and vanilla extract. Process until thick and sticky.

Form the mixture into 1-inch balls by rolling small portions between your palms. Place the balls directly on a serving tray or into a wide, flat storage container as you make each one. Serve immediately, or refrigerate until ready to serve.

Per ball: calories: 71, protein: 2 g, fat: 451 g, carbohydrate: 5 g, fiber: 1.5 g, sodium: 1 mg

Cocoa Balls: Add 1 tablespoon of unsweetened cocoa powder or carob powder to the food processor when you add the dates.

Snowballs: Put about 1 cup of unsweetened shredded dried coconut in a flat dish and roll the Bliss Balls in the coconut until thoroughly coated.

Tahini Chews

YIELD: *about 36 chews*

Although these chews contain wholesome ingredients, beware of the addicting flavor. They're very easy to put together, and you actually don't even have to cook them. One day I only had time to bake about half of a batch, so I refrigerated the remaining batter, intending to finish the job the next day. A few days later while perusing the refrigerator, it occurred to me that I could simply eat the stuff raw. I did. And it was good. That's one of the reasons I don't call these cookies.

½ cup tahini
½ cup agave nectar
1½ cups rolled oats
⅓ cup dried cherries, raisins, or dried cranberries

Preheat the oven to 350 degrees F. Line a baking sheet with parchment paper.

Put the tahini and agave nectar in a large bowl. Stir until thoroughly combined. Stir in the oats and cherries. Drop the batter onto the prepared baking sheet using a teaspoon.

Bake for 10 minutes. Let the chews cool on the baking sheet for 10 minutes. Transfer to a wire rack to cool completely.

Per chew: calories: 50, protein: 1 g, fat: 2 g, carbohydrate: 7 g, fiber: 1 g, sodium: 3 mg

Peanut Butter Chews: Use peanut butter in place of the tahini and increase the agave nectar to ⅔ cup.

Soft Chews: Use quick-cooking oats in place of the rolled oats.

Chocolate Mousse

YIELD: *4 servings*

Perfectly ripe avocados form the creamy base for this chocolate mousse sweetened with agave nectar and brightened with a bit of lime juice.

2 ripe Hass avocados
¾ cup agave nectar
½ cup unsweetened cocoa powder
2 teaspoons freshly squeezed lime juice
Optional: ½ to 2 teaspoons vanilla extract (see tip)

Combine all of the ingredients in a food processor. Process until completely smooth, stopping at least twice to scrape down the sides of the work bowl. Serve immediately, or transfer to a storage container and refrigerate until ready to serve.

Per serving: calories: 395, protein: 6 g, fat: 17 g, carbohydrate: 56 g, fiber: 12 g, sodium: 6 mg

Tip: Taste the mousse without the vanilla extract. If you're delighted, leave it as is. If you think it needs an extra bit of flavoring, add the vanilla extract to taste.

Peach Sauce

YIELD: *3/4 cup*

This lightly sweetened fruit sauce can be served over pies, fresh fruit, or creamy frozen desserts, as well as over waffles, pancakes, or crêpes.

¼ cup agave nectar
1 teaspoon cornstarch
⅛ teaspoon ground ginger
1 cup frozen peach chunks

Combine the agave nectar, cornstarch, and ginger in a small saucepan and mix well. Stir in the peaches. Cook over medium-low heat, stirring frequently, for 5 to 7 minutes, or until the mixture bubbles and thickens. Serve immediately, or for a thicker sauce, cool before serving.

Per 2 tablespoons: calories: 53, protein: 0 g, fat: 0 g, carbohydrate: 13 g, fiber: 0.5 g, sodium: 0 mg

Banana Split: Slice a banana lengthwise and place it in an oblong dish. Top with ½ cup of vegan vanilla ice cream, 2 tablespoons of Peach Sauce, and 1 tablespoon of chopped nuts.

Cashew Crème

YIELD: *1½ cups*

This luscious and sophisticated crème has a subtle flavor, making it extremely versatile. Spoon it over fresh berries or pie, enjoy it as is with a sprig of fresh mint for garnish, or, for an elegant dessert, layer the it with fresh blackberries in a dainty dessert bowl.

1 package (12.3 ounces) firm silken tofu
¼ cup cashew butter
¼ cup agave nectar, or more as needed
2 teaspoons vanilla extract

Put the tofu in a food processor. Process until completely smooth, stopping at least once to scrape down the sides of the work bowl. Add the cashew butter, agave nectar, and vanilla extract. Process until completely smooth. Add more agave nectar to taste, if desired. Serve immediately, or transfer to a storage container and refrigerate until ready to serve. The crème will firm up a bit as it chills.

Per 2 tablespoons: calories: 71, protein: 3 g, fat: 3 g, carbohydrate: 8 g, fiber: 0 g, sodium: 11 mg

Chocolate Crème

YIELD: *2½ cups*

Incredibly versatile, Chocolate Crème can be a mousse (or a pudding, depending on the age of the person eating it), a layer in a rich and chocolaty parfait with strawberries and raspberries, the basis of a chocolate cream pie, or even the filling in cupcakes or a cake. In short, it's divine enough to use in many different ways, all of which will satisfy your inner chocoholic.

1 package (12.3 ounces) firm silken tofu
⅓ cup agave nectar
1 tablespoon vanilla extract
1 cup vegan chocolate chips

Put the tofu in a food processor. Process for at least 2 minutes, until smooth, stopping at least once to scrape down the sides of the work bowl. Add the agave nectar and vanilla extract. Process until smooth. Leave the mixture in the food processor.

Pour about 2 inches of water into a large skillet. Bring to a simmer over medium heat. Put the chocolate chips in a heatproof bowl or saucepan. Set the bowl in the simmering water. Stir the chocolate chips for about 5 minutes, or until melted and completely smooth.

Lift the bowl out of the simmering water and dry the bottom of the bowl. Use a rubber spatula to transfer the chocolate to the food processor. Process until thoroughly combined, stopping at least once to scrape down the sides of the work bowl. Serve immediately, or transfer to a storage container and refrigerate until ready to serve. The crème will firm up a bit as it chills.

Per 2 tablespoons: calories: 73, protein: 2 g, fat: 3 g, carbohydrate: 10 g, fiber: 0 g, sodium: 6 mg

Black Russian Crème: Add 1 tablespoon of coffee liqueur when you add the vanilla extract.

Chocolate Cream Pie: Replace the firm silken tofu with extra-firm silken tofu. Spoon the mixture into a prebaked graham cracker crust and smooth the top with the back of the spoon. Refrigerate for at least 6 hours before serving.

Cheesecake Crème

YIELD: *1 3/4 cups*

This creamy dessert sauce is so adaptable. Serve it in a bowl surrounded by fresh strawberries for dipping, drizzle it over bowl of blueberries, use it as a strawberry shortcake topping, or make a parfait in a glass dessert dish by alternating it with layers of fresh fruit.

1 container (8 ounces) vegan cream cheese
½ cup firm or extra-firm silken tofu
½ cup organic sugar
2 teaspoons vanilla extract

Combine the cream cheese and tofu in a food processor. Process for about 2 minutes, until smooth and creamy, stopping at least once to scrape down the sides of the work bowl. Add the sugar and vanilla extract. Process until smooth and creamy. Transfer to a storage container and refrigerate for at least 1 hour before serving.

Per 2 tablespoons: calories: 81, protein: 1 g, fat: 4 g, carbohydrate: 9 g, fiber: 0 g, sodium: 55 mg

Ice Cream Dream Bars

YIELD: *15 to 24 bars*

These fun and frosty treats offer instant summertime relief, and I guarantee no one will have any trouble eating them before they melt. Chocolate ice cream is particularly tasty in this recipe, but you can let your imagination run wild.

1 jar (18 ounces, or 1½ cups) crunchy unsalted peanut butter (with no added oil)
½ cup agave nectar
3 cups crispy rice cereal
1 quart vegan ice cream, softened at room temperature for about 30 minutes

Lightly mist an 8 x 11-inch baking pan with nonstick cooking spray.

Put the peanut butter and agave nectar in a large bowl and mix until thoroughly combined. Gently stir in the cereal. Press the mixture into the prepared pan, using damp fingertips to spread it evenly over the bottom of the pan.

Using a large spoon, dot the ice cream over the peanut butter mixture and use the back of a spoon to spread it in an even layer. Cover with plastic wrap and freeze for at least 4 hours. Cut into squares before serving.

Per bar: calories: 231, protein: 7 g, fat: 14 g, carbohydrate: 21 g, fiber: 3 g, sodium: 68 mg

INDEX

BOOK PUBLISHING COMPANY

since 1974—books that educate, inspire, and empower

To find your favorite vegetarian and soyfood products online, visit:
www.healthy-eating.com

Local Bounty
Seasonal Vegan Recipes
Devra Gartenstein
978-1-57067-219-4

**The Simple Little Vegan
Slow Cooker**
Michelle Rivera
978-1-57067-251-4

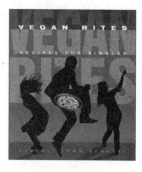

Vegan Bites
Recipes for Singles
Beverly Lynn Bennett
978-1-57067-221-7

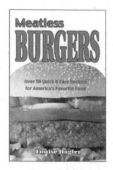

Meatless Burgers
*Over 50 Quick & Easy Recipies
for America's Favorite Food*
Louise Hagler
978-1-57067-087-9

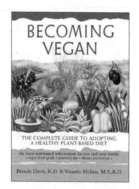

Becoming Vegan
Brenda Davis, RD,
Vesanto Melina, MS, RD
978-1-57067-103-6

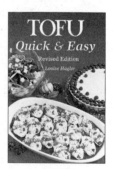

Tofu, Quick & Easy
Revised Edition
Louise Hagler
978-1-57067-112-8

Purchase these health titles and cookbooks from your local bookstore
or natural food store, or you can buy them directly from:

Book Publishing Company • P.O. Box 99 • Summertown, TN 38483
1-800-695-2241

Please include $3.95 per book for shipping and handling.